2020 Rat Year
Feng Shui Planner

January 2020 to February 2021

by **Picturehealer**
Shih-Tien Wu

www.picturehealer.com
https://www.youtube.com/c/picturehealer

Table of Content

Part 1

Part 2

The Feng Shui Lunisolar Calendar & Planner

www.picturehealer.com
https://www.youtube.com/c/picturehealer

2020 Rat Year Overview & Ba Zi Analysis

The rat is the first animal sign in the Chinese zodiac and 2020 marks the beginning of a new cycle. It is a good year to look at your long term goals and what you really want in the next 10 to 20 years. We can do this by using the Rat year 4 pillar chart, the annual Flying Star chart, and the Chinese horoscope for the 12 animal signs.

We tend to care too much about what others think and lose our dreams when we get older. What you enjoy doing most as a little kid usually reflects your strengths and passion. However, it's never too late to pursue your dreams. With this New Year, it's time to rekindle your passion and start planning again.

The Ba Zi chart of the 2020 Rat year is like a person's birth chart. Below is the chart based on the Li Chun (beginning of spring) date, 2/04/2020.

2/04/2020 Li Chun 立春 (Beginning of Spring)

	Hour	Day	Month	Year
Heavenly Stem	**Ji 己**	**Ding 丁**	**Wu 戊**	**Geng 庚**
	Yin Earth	Yin Fire	Yang Earth	Yang Metal
Earthly Branch	**You 酉**	**Chou 丑**	**Yin 寅**	**Zi 子**
	Yin Metal	Yin Earth	Yang Wood	Yang Water
	Rooster	*Ox*	*Tiger*	*Rat*

4 Pillar chart / Ba Zi 八字

(1)

The Year Piller: Metal Generates Water

Yang Metal Qualities:
The Yang Metal is related to a warrior, fighter, commander, or leader. Somone with a strong will and aggressive temper. The focus is on Finance and Technology.

Yang Water Qualities:
Water represents flexibility, fast acting, money flow, relationship and romance. It looks soft and harmless, but can be very powerful.

The strong element of the Rat year

#1 The strongest: **Metal**

#2. The second strongest: **Water**

#3. The third: **Earth**

#4. The weak: **Fire**

#5. The weakest: **Wood**

The strongest/ lucky colors of the 2020 Rat Year

Metal colors:
Gold, silver, white, or any shiny, metallic colors.

Water colors:
Any shades of blue, black, or clear.

The 5 element and business industry

Metal:
- Finance, banking, insurance, gold/precious metal, machinery, technology, engineering, military, and police.

Water:
- Tourism, beverage, restaurant, retailing, communication, or anything to do with the sea and water.

Earth:
- Real estate, architecture, construction, antique, pottery. mining, or anything to do with the earth, soil, and land.

Fire:
- Artist, designer, computer, electronics, gas/oil/petroleum, or anything related to the use of the light, heat and fuel.

Wood:
- Author, journalist, publisher, teacher, furniture, textile, garment/fashion, healthcare, library, bookshop, office supply, or anything related to trees, plants, fiber, and paper.

The business related to the Metal and Water will see a stronger growth in the 2020 year of the Rat.

A year of the Peach Blossom and helpful people luck

The Water/Rat year also means
a year of **Romance/Peach blossom luck** 桃花
and helpful people **(Gui Ren)** 貴人

Rat, Horse, Rooster, and Rabbit are 4 animal signs strongly related to **romance**.

The Rat year will show the increased focus on the *personal and public relationship including romance, helpful people (Nobleman or Gui Ren), business relationship, and social media.*

Beauty, personal branding, and entertainment business will also be highlighted in 2020.

Character of a Rat

- Very social
- **Sensitive**
- Witty and smart
- **Enjoy good food/drink**
- Like to hide treasures
- **Fast acting, proactive**
- Adaptable & flexible
- **Family oriented**
- Hard working
- **Easily scared**
- Can be stubborn
- **Can be worrisome**

To take advantage of the Rat year, we can learn from these little animals.

Try to be **flexible, fast acting, work hard, take care of our family, help each other, and grow tsogether.**

2020 Rat Year
Annual Flying Star Chart

2020 Flying Star chart

South

	3 killings Sui Po (year breaker)	
Southeast		Southwest
6 White	**2 Black**	**4 Green**
East **5 Yellow**	**7 Red**	**9 Purple** West
Northeast **1 White**	**3 Jade** Tai Shui (Grand duke)	**8 White** Northwest

North

Period 8 (2004 - 2023)

Upcoming auspicious stars: # 9, #1

Current lucky star: #8

Outdated star: **#7** (mixed)

Weak stars: **#2, #6**

Conflicting stars: **#3, #4, #5**

Auspicious

↓

Inauspicious

1 - 2 - 3 - 4 - 5 - 6 - 7 - 8 - 9

✓   ✗ ✗ ✗   ✓ ✓

1 White Star (Northeast in 2020)

Also called the "Tan Lang" 貪狼 star and "Wen Chang" star. **Water** element. **1 White star** is related to literature, art, intelligence, promotion, fame, social status, popularity, and career advancement.

The **Northeast** belongs to the **Earth** element. *Earth is controlling Water,* so there is a tendency of **urinary/ kidney** problem especially for the **middle boy child** or **middle age male.**

Add more **Metal element** such as **white color** or **metal decoration** here to *generate more water and balance out too much Earth element.*

Since this is the **Wen Chang** location, it is good for *study room, office, or bedroom.* Place "Wen Chang Pagoda" or "Chinese brush set" to activate the *intelligence and promotion luck.*

2 Black Star (South in 2020)

Also called "Ju Men" 巨門 star. **Earth** element.
2 Black star represents illness, accident, quarrel, or financial loss.

South belongs to **Fire element.** *Fire generates Earth* so it strengthens the #2 star. South is also related to **middle daughter** and **fire related disease.** Watch out for **heart, small intestine, and inflammation problem,** especially for *middle daughter or middle-age women.*

Water element such as black/ blue color can balance between the Earth and Fire energy and reduce the #2 star's negative energy.

Feng Shui cures for #2 star are similar to #5 star because both are Earth element. Metal objects can reduce the Earth energy of the #2 star. **Use bronze Hulu (for health and reduce negative Qi), 5 Emperor's coin, brass/bronze Pi Xiu or Qi Lin.**

In 2020, **The Three Killings (San Sha) and Yearbreaker (Sui Po) are both in the South. So avoid renovation here in 2020.** Avoid sitting on the South side.

3 Jade Star (North in 2020)

Also called "Lu Cun" 祿存 star. Wood element.

3 Jade stars represents **quarrel, dispute, or legal issue.** #3 star can bring prosperity and fame in the right time but period 8 is not the best time for the 3 Jade star.

·······

North belongs to the **Water element. Water generates Wood** so it is a compatible location.

To reduce the negative power of #3 star (Wood), apply **Metal element** (*white, silver, gold....*) **to control the Wood,** or **Fire element** such as *red, purple, or orange* color to reduce the Wood. **Avoid plants and green colors (Wood) here to reduce the #3 star.**

In 2020, North is also the location of *Tai Shui (Grand Duke of Jupiter)* so **avoid facing North direction when sitting down,** and **avoid renovation** in the North part of the house.

Pi Xiu is the best Feng Shui cure for Tai Shui. Tai Shui plague/amulet/card is another traditional cure.

Displaying natural **crystals** can enhance the energy of the space. **Laughing buddha** can reduce the fighting energy.

4 Green Star (Southwest in 2020)

Also called "Wen Qu" 文曲 star. Wood element.

4 Green star is related to study, art, literature, culture, and career advance. It is also related to **romance (Peach blossom), social life, and emotional well-being.**

·······

Southwest belongs to the **Earth** element. *Wood controls the Earth* so **we can add Fire element (red, purple, orange) to balance out the energy.**

Since this is the "**Wen Chang 文昌**" location, you can **display *4 lucky bamboo*** (for #4 star), *Chinese ink brush,* or *Wen Chang Pagoda* **to enhance your intelligence and exam/promotion luck.**

Place *rose quartz, amethyst,* or *a pair of Mandarin ducks* for *relationship luck.*

In Period 8, # 4 star is not a timely star so the *negative side effect* can be **relationship trouble** *(rotton peach blossom luck)* or **emotional problem.**

5 Yellow Star (East in 2020)

Also called "**Lian Zhen**" 廉貞 star. Earth element.

5 Yellow is the **number 1 negative star**. It relates to **accident, money loss, fire, ghost, and all kind of misfortune**. It is best to **avoid renovation** or too much activity here.

East belongs to the **Wood element**. *Wood controls the Earth* so **the power of 5 yellow star is reduced here.**

Avoid important areas in the East such as main entrance, living room, kitchen, or bedroom. **No renovation in the East in 2020 Rat year** to avoid disturbing the 5 Yellow star.

Similar to the #2 Black star Feng Shui cure, **use Metal element to reduce the negative of the Earth energy. Use *white, silver, golden colors, metal furniture, bronze/brass Hu Lu, clock with metal pendulum, 5 element pagoda, metal windchime* or *symbol of Qian*** (3 unbroken lines in the Ba Gua, meaning the most yang and heaven).

Reduce Earth element (less yellow, brown, or plants with soil) here.

6 White Star (Southeast in 2020)

Also called "**Wu Qu**" 武曲 star. Metal element.

6 White star is related to **authority, career promotion, wealth, and mentor luck**. It is not a timely star in period 8, so #6 star can show as **stubborn, reckless, or controlling behavior, and lawsuit, accident, or financial loss.**

Southeast belongs to the **Wood element**. *Metal controls the Wood* so it is a conflicting relationship. It tends to affect **oldest daughter** most. Watch out for **liver, gallbladder, and eye problems** *(Wood type disease in Chinese medicine).*

Water element can harmonize Metal and Wood *(Metal generates Water and Water generates Wood).* **Display black or blue furnishing or water feature such as a *fish tank.***

6 White star is **also a money star. You can set up a money altar (treasure chest) here with *5 emperor's coin, crystal, Qi Lin, Pi Xiu,* or *Money Toad*.** Display *Quan Yin statue* for mentor luck and protection. Since #6 is not a timely star, **watch out for sharp metal objects and avoid gambling.**

7 Red Star (Center in 2020)

Also called the "Po Jun" 破軍 star. Metal element.
7 Red star is related to communication, mass media, quarrel, fighting, accidents related to fire or knife/sword. In the body, it's related to the lung, respiratory system, and large intestine.

The **Center** belongs to the **Earth** element. **Earth generates Metal,** so it is a good location for the #7 star. However, #7 star **is outdated in the Period 8** so it *does not bring strong luck.*

Avoid sharp metal or triangle shape objects in this area to *prevent accident.* Be careful about get into **a fight or quarrel.**

Water can reduce the Metal element. Add a **fish tank, water plant, or water fountain** to soften the strong Metal energy. Use the colors of water to decorate: **black, blue.**

Display black or blue **crystals** or jade **Quan Yin** to enhance the energy.

8 White Star (Northwest in 2020)

Also called the "Zuo Fu" 左辅 star. Earth element. 8 White star is the **number 1 money star.** Since we are in Period 8, it is **the timely star.** It's related to **fame, prosparity, longevity, career, real-estate, and offpring luck.**

The **Northwest** belongs to the **Metal** element. **Earth** generates **Metal,** so it is a good location for the #8 star. #8 star **is the most auspicious star in the Period 8** so take full advantage and **setup important spaces (master bedroom, living room, office, kitchen...) here.**

To **activate the wealth luck,** place **ceramic vase, yellow crystal, or money jars** to enhance the **Earth element** of the number 8 star. Use earth color of **yellow, brown, or beige.**

If you have **too much Metal** element in your birth chart, you can **reduce white, gold, silver color or display less metal objects here.** Too much **Metal** can weaken the **Earth.**

9 Purple Star (West in 2020)

Also called the "You Bi" 右弼 star. Fire element. Number 9 Purple star is related to the festive event, rising energy, and wealth. It's also related to helpful people (Gui Ren), love relationship (peach blossom), and real estate luck. On the other side, it can be related to heart, eye, blood vessel problem, or fire and accident.

West belongs to the Metal element. Fire controls Metal, so there can be stress and indecision (especially affect young girls). Metal is related to lung and large intestine, so watch out for compromised respiratory diseases.

The solution is to add more Metal element. Use white, silver, gold colors. Display metal objects or electronics.

Earth element is also very good here. Earth reduces too much fire and also generates Metal. Use earth colors (yellow, brown, beige...) and earthware (ceramic, pottery...). Use purple and red to enhance the #9 Purple star.

Since this is a money star, you can set up a money altar here and display money jar, Qi Lin, Pi Xiu, money toad, and other auspicious items to attract wealth.

Best areas in 2020 Rat year

1 White star: Northeast
8 White star: Northwest
9 Purple Star: West

Northeast, Northwest, and West are the most auspicious areas in 2020 Chinese Rat year.

- Set up **important rooms** in these areas.
- Stay in these areas **longer**.
- Add enhancers such as **Pi Xiu, Qi Lin, dragon, crystal, and jade for propsperity and good fortune.**

No construction areas in 2020 Rat year

3 Killings (San Sha): South
Year Breaker (Sui Po): South
Tai Shui (Grand Duke Jupiter): North
5 Yellow Star: East
2 Black Star: South

North and South are not auspicious directions in the Rat year.
East (5 Yellow) is also *inauspicious.*

- Avoid staying in these areas for too long.
- **No contruction** or noisy movement here.
- Relocate or re-arrange furnitures if necessary.
- Place at least *one cure* in these areas for protection.

12 Animal signs horoscope for the 2020 Rat Year

The yearly animal sign starts on the
Li Chun (Start of Spring),
usually falls on the 2/04 of the Western
calendar.

立春

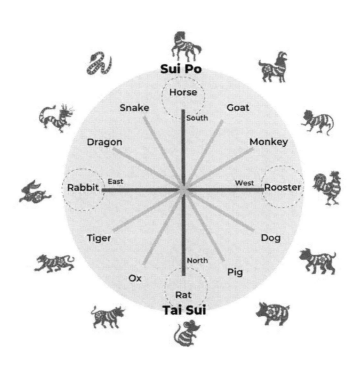

12 Animal signs horoscope for the 2020 Rat Year

1. Rat

There are 2 positive stars to bring you **authority, leadership, and income** this year. With these lucky stars, career and income are above average.

2 negative stars might cause **health problem or accident**. Watch out when *operating machine or handle sharp objects*.

Since this is your **"Tai Sui year"**, you feel the *stressful and unstable energy*. It is best to **be conservative, avoid quarrel and conflict, avoid impulse spending and risky investment.**

To counter the Tai Sui, the best way is to **have big festive evenets this year (wedding, baby) or attending other's festive events. Do more charity work will also increase your luck.**

2. Ox

The Ox is one of the *most lucky* signs in 2020 Rat year. The "6 harmony" star **indicating festive event and career achievement.**

There is a star indicating travel and move/change in career is favorable.

Helpful people (Gui Ren) are on your side when needed. You can meet the right teacher, mentor, or boss. It is a good year to build your team for support. Great luck in relationship. Singles can expect to meet the right person.

There is a **Tai Yang (sun) star** indicating **male energy is strong. Male Ox has better luck than female this year.** Female Ox should be careful about *relationship trouble, and avoid gossip about others.*

There is an **illness star.** Take care of your health, watch your stress level, and maintain proper diet.

3. Tiger

There is a **"heavenly dog" star** indicating the **chance of traveling** far away from home. It also means working hard, and unexpected spending to fix broken items. Be careful about travel related health problems.

Since there is no lucky stars this year, **tigers need to rely on themselves. Pay attention to details** to avoid mistakes. **Be conservative,** avoid fighting with authority, avoid risky investment and impulse spending.

A star indicating **illness and injury. Avoid visiting hospital or attending funeral.** On the other hand, **attending more festive events** and do **more charity work** to increase your luck.

4. Rabbit

Rabbit has the best love relationship luck of all signs this year. Increased **chance of happy marriage or having babies** this year.

Helpful people (Gui Ren) are surrounding Rabbit including friends, superiors, business partners... Good luck in career and fame.

Female Rabbit has better luck than male Rabbit this year. Male rabbit needs to watch out relationship problem *(rotten peach blossom)*.

A star indicating gossip and problems from negative people **(Xiao Ren)**. Try to **communicate clearly, avoid talking behind others, and avoid conflict or argument.**

Social spending can drain your pocket, and be conservative in money management. Rabbit is also *affected by Tai Sui in 2020*, so **attending festive event and do more charity work to increase luck.**

Dragon

In 2020, there are **several lucky stars** indicating **great luck at career, fame, and money.**

There will be **increased authority and high chance of promotion.** There is a *"Golden cabinet" star* to help you **accumulate money** this year. It is a good year to take your career to the next level and invest actively. Students have good exam luck too.

Love relationship is not bad either. The *"Three haromny" star* brings you **helpful people** (Gui Ren) and good friends. **Watch for jealous people** causing trouble behind you.

On the negative side, there is a **"White tiger" star** that might cause health issue, injury or accident.
The traditional way to counter the **"White tiger" star** is similar with the **"Tai Sui" star. Go to a temple during the beginning of the new year to pray for a peaceful year,** and *do more charity and volunteer work. Donate blood and money.*

Snake

In the past few years, Snake has been struggling a lot but 2020 is a very lucky year for you. **A lot of lucky stars go to your sign this year so it is time to wake up from your hibernation and be the star.**

Your **career is going to a new height** in 2020 Rat year. **Helpful people (Gui Ren)** show up at the right time to solve any problems. It is also a good time to **start your business or change career.**

Income, fame, status will be increased in 2020. Students have good luck learning new skills and **passing exams.**

Since everything is going your way, you feel *confident and charming.* That helps to build **a happy love relationship and social life. Overall health is good this year too.**

There are some minor negative stars for snakes. **Watch out for legal trouble, avoid being a guarantor for friends, and keep the work/life balance.**

Horse

Horse is opposite to the "**Tai Sui**" **Rat** position in 2020. It has a negative star "**Sui Po**" (year breaker) that might indicate **the waste of money/effort and unstable luck.** This is a challenging year for horses.

There are more negative stars than lucky stars for horse in 2020 Rat year. **Career tends to be slow and frustrating. There might be unexpeced spending and money wasted.**

This is the year to **stay low-key, be conservative, and be careful of what you say** to avoid trouble and fighting. **Keep your emotion calm and cool. Avoid making impulsive decisions.**

Take good care of your health and your family's health. It is time to enrich yourself and build your strength instead of going out and be a hero.

 If you can plan some **festive event** or **attend other's wedding or birthday party, the happy energy can drive away many minor troubles.** Be patient and your year to shine will come soon.

Goat

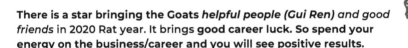

There is a star bringing the Goats *helpful people (Gui Ren) and good friends* in 2020 Rat year. It brings **good career luck. So spend your energy on the business/career and you will see positive results.**

There is a star indicating **minor money loss or unexpected spending.** Be conservative in money management. **Save money for emergency and avoid big investment in 2020.**

For love relationsip, single goats have good chances of **meeting older/upper class people.**

There is a star associated with **health problem or accident.** Avoid visiting sick patients at hospital or attending funerals. Attending happy events such as wedding or birthday party can raise your happy energy and drive away troubles.

Watch your health, stay positive, and the the lucky star will resolve any problems you might have this year.

Monkey

Monkey's luck increases in 2020 compared to 2019. The best areas are **career, money, and social life because of the "Three harmony" star.**

Being smart and adaptable, monkeys can easily get a promotion or be in charge at work in 2020 year of the rat. Your authority and fame increase this year. You also have **helpful people** supporting you at work and social life.

You can accumulate wealth quickly because of the "**golden cabinet**" star. But there is also a star indicating **money loss because of helping friends.**

Most trouble comes from **negative friends and jealous people (Xiao Ren)** in 2020. Be careful about what you say, avoid casual jokes or gossip. A friendly relationship is more important than being the right one.

 # Rooster

Rooster has **good relationship luck in 2020 (peach blossom luck). It is a good year to get married or have a baby because of the lucky "heavenly happiness" star.** Married Rooster can benefit from the increased popularity at work or personal life.

You have a **"Tai Yin" star** indicating **better luck for female roosters** this year. **Female friends** can give you helpful advices if needed. **Male rooster should watch out for female trouble or gossip.**

Becuause of your good relationship and the support of **helpful people (Gui Ren), career and money are a little slow but growing steadily.**

It is a good idea to be conservative and focus on enrich yourself. Improve your skills, exercise reguarly, and keep a positive mind.

Dog

2020 Rat year is **a smooth year for dog signs.** You start to see the result from hard work of past few years. **Business is your strong area this year.** There is a star indicating **success when travel far from home.**

Dogs have improved fame, status and money in 2020. It is a good year to show your ambition, work hard, and invest wisely. **Students have good luck at exams too.**

There is a star showing **indicision and doubt. Keep a positive attitude and stay optimistic.**

Love relationship is steady and no big change. Pay attention to better communication.

Some minor negative stars related to **health.** Watch for **travel related accidents.** Don't forget your **routine health checkup.**

Pig

2020 is the year of **money, work, and relationship luck for pigs.** Pig conflicts with *Tai Sui* in 2019 Pig year. Your feel less stressed in 2020.

There is a "Tai Yang" (the sun) star indicating **great fortune at career. You enjoy increased fame and social status. You can see increased money luck** especially if you have your own business.

You have good **peach blossom (love relationship) luck** this year. You are popular and leave people good impressions. However, watch for the "**rotten peach blossom**" from unwanted relationship. Keep your proper boundary to avoid trouble.

There is a minor star indicating **unrealistic ideas and empty promise.** Remind yourself to work step by step from the ground up.

Tips to increase your luck

If you are *very lucky* this year,

There might be *jealous people (Xiao Ren)* trying to cause trouble behind you. So **watch your attitude. Avoid gossip or get involved in little groups. Be generous and polite.**

If you are leading a team, **try to understand other's point of view** instead of just give orders.

Health might be compromised because of the hardwork and stress. Don't forget the proper diet and exercise.

When you are in good luck, it is easy to forget the less fortunate people. **Don't forget to give back by donating money, time, and your influence.**

If you are *not very lucky* this year,

It is **time to be conservative and focus on building your skills and health. Time to learn more and listen to other expert's advice.**

Watch your diet, exercise, and mental health. **A positive attitude can make a big difference.** When the lucky stars align with your sign next time, you will be ready to go.

Take care of your famiy and close friends. Take care of the weaker ones and ask advices from the lucky ones. **We all influence each other and share the luck.** Maybe have someone with better luck join your team and borrow their strength.

Don't forget to **build up your Karma by charity work, doing good deeds, and help those in need.**

Lastly, **plan some happy events or attend happy events such as a wedding or birthday party** to bring up you lucky energy.

How to use the Feng Shui calendar

Element of the day

Use the 5 element relationship to enhance or reduce certain energy

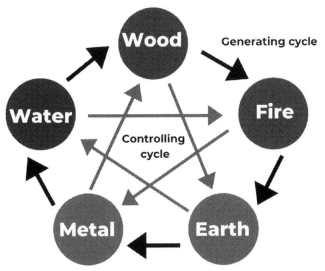

Lucky Directions of the day
The **Festive God** & **Wealth God** location of the day

- If you have choices, go to these lucky directions of the day for extra luck.

- Or, travel toward one of these 2 directions first before you continue your intended direction.

- The first direction is the location of the Festive God, the second direction is the Money God. Follow the Money God direction if that is your goal, or Festive God direction for general happiness.

- For example, pick a restaurant or seating in one of the lucky directions for lunch or meeting.

Conflicting animal sign and direction of the day

When picking up a day for your important event, make sure the most important people involved is not the conflicting animal sign of the day. In that case, it is better to pick a different.

Each animal sign has a corrosponding direction. Avoid that conflicting direction of the day for important event if possible.

Common activities and terms

A
- Activating a statue
- Adopting animals

B
- Bathing

C
- Ceremony
- Cleaning the house

D
- Dressmaking
- Demolition of a house

F
- Fixing street/walkway or walls
- Funeral
- Fishing

H
- Haircut
- Hunting

M
- Moving
- Moving to a new house

P
- Planting
- Pest control

R
- Removing (Feng Shui cures)

S
- Starting a business
- Starting a construction
- Signing a contract
- Setting up a bed/door/stove

T
- Trading

V
- Visiting a doctor

W
- Wedding

Activitiy Terms
The original meaning & the modern interpretation

Ceremony
old - religious ritual for the god or ancestor at home or temple
new - any ritual, praying or meditation.

Bathing
old - purifying your body to prepare for a ceremony or an important event.
new - any bathing or spa.

Haircut
old- for baby's first haircut or the head-shaving for nun/monks.
new- any haircut.

Dress Making
old - tailoring formal garments for big events such as a wedding or funeral.
new - dress making for important events.

Demolition of a house
old- taking down unwanted part of a building.
new - the same.

Fixing a street/walkway/wall
old - repairing street, public space, or exterior of a building.
new - repairing a driveway, renovating the exterior of a building.

House Cleaning
old - deep cleaning of the interior of a house, get rid of anything outdated.
new - the same.

Visiting a doctor
old - treating any health issues, getting an acupuncture.
new - the same.

Removing a Feng Shui cure
old - house cleaning or ceremony to remove any negative energy in the house, including removing related cure, charm, or religious items.
new - remove/disgard Feng Shui cure, charm, or religious items when no longer needed.

Activating a statue
old - a religious ceremony to activate a buddha or other sculpture, usually involving painting or dotting the eyes. (The eye-opening ceremony)
new - activating a Feng Shui cure, personal charm, or religious object with a prayer or ceremony.

Starting a business
old - 1. opening a new store for business or,
2. re-opening the store/shop after long holidays.
new - the same.

Starting a construction
old - the first day of starting a construction project.
new - the same

Setting up a bed/door/stove
old - setting up a new bed/door/stove or re-arranging them according to the Feng Shui principle.
new - the same.

Planting
old - farming and growing crops.
new - any gardening activity.

Pest Control
old - catching pests, destructive animals, and bugs to protect the crops and house. It can include filling up ant's nest holes and treating termites.
new - general pest control around the house.

Wedding
old - various activities related to the wedding including asking permission for marriage, discussing the money/gift, engagement and wedding ceremony.
new - wedding and engagement ceremony.

Funeral
old - various activities related to the funeral including the funeral ceremony, burial, cremation, or fixing a tomb.
new - funeral ceremony and related activities.

Meeting friends
old - gathering with friends and family.
new - social gathering, meeting, and partying.

Travel
old - long trip away from home
new - any trip, especially for air trips.

24 Solar Terms (Jie Qi)

2020 / 2021 Date	Chinese term	Meaning
1. January 6 / January 05	Xiao Han 小寒	Slight Cold
2. January 20 / January 20	Da Han 大寒	Great Cold
3. February 04 / February 03	Li Chun 立春	Beginning of Spring
4. February 19 / February 18	Yu Shui 雨水	Rain Water
5. March 05	Jing Xhe 驚蟄	Waking of Insects
6. March 20	Chun Fen 春分	Spring Equinox
7. April 04	Qing Ming 清明	Clear and Bright
8. April 19	Gu Yu 穀雨	Grain Rain
9. May 05	Li Xia 立夏	Beginning of Summer
10. May 20	Xiao Man 小滿	Slight Mature
11. June 05	Mang Zhong 芒種	Planting Grains
12. June 21	Xia Zhi 夏至	Summer Solstice
13. July 06	Xiao Shu 小暑	Slight Heat
14. July 22	Da Shu 大暑	Great Heat
15. August 07	Li Qiu 立秋	Beginning of Autumn
16. August 22	Chu Shu 處暑	End of Summer
17. September 07	Bai Lu 白露	White Dew
18. September 22	Qiu Fen 秋分	Autumn Equinox
19. October 08	Han Lu 寒露	Cold Dew
20. October 23	Shuang Jiang 霜降	Frost Falling
21. November 07	Li Dong 立冬	Beginning of Winter
22. November 22	Xiao Xue 小雪	Slight Snow
23. December 07	Da Xue 大雪	Great Snow
24. December 21	Dong Zhi 冬至	Winter Solstice

The Heavenly Stems
& Earthly Branches

10 Heavenly Stems

1. **Jia** Yang Wood
2. **Yi** Yin Wood
3. **Bing** Yang Fire
4. **Ding** Yin Fire
5. **Wu** Yang Earth
6. **Ji** Yin Earth
7. **Geng** Yang Metal
8. **Xin** Yin Metal
9. **Ren** Yang Water
10. **Kui** Yin Water

12 Earthly Branches

1. **Zi** Rat Yang Water
2. **Chou** Ox Yin Earth
3. **Yin** Tiger Yang Wood
4. **Mao** Rabbit Yin Wood
5. **Chen** Dragoon Yang Earth
6. **Si** Snake Yin Fire
7. **Wu** Horse Yang Fire
8. **Wei** Goat Yin Earth
9. **Shen** Monkey Yang Metal
10. **You** Rooster Yin Metal
11. **Xu** Dog Yang Earth
12. **Hai** Pig Yin Water

The 10 Heavenly Stems and 12 Earthly Branches creates 60 combinations.

In 2020, it is the year of "Geng Zi" (Yang Metal, Yang Water)
In 2021, it is the year of "Xin Chou"(Yin Metal, Yin Earth)

January 2020

Monday	Tuesday	Wednesday	Thursday
		1 (lunar: 12/07/19)	**2** (11/08/19)
6 Xiao Han (11/12/19)	**7** (11/13/19)	**8** (11/14/19)	**9** (11/15/19)
13 (lunar 12/19/19)	**14** (12/20/19)	**15** (12/21/19)	**16** (12/22/19)
20 Da Han (12/26/19)	**21** (12/27/19)	**22** (12/28/19)	**23** (12/29/19)
27 (1/03/20)	**28** (1/04/20)	**29** (1/05/20)	**30** (1/06/20)

Friday	Saturday	Sunday	Goals
3 (11/09/19)	**4** (11/10/19)	**5** (11/11/19)	
10 (11/16/19)	**11** (11/17/19)	**12** (11/18/19)	
17 (12/23/19)	**18** (12/24/19)	**19** (12/25/19)	
24 (12/30/19)	**25** * Chinese New Year (lunar 1/01/20)	**26** (1/02/20)	
31 (1/07/20)			

February 2020

Monday	Tuesday	Wednesday	Thursday
3 (1/10)	**4** Li Chun (1/11)	**5** (1/12)	**6** (1/13)
10 (1/17)	**11** (1/18)	**12** (1/19)	**13** (1/20)
17 (1/24)	**18** (1/25)	**19** Yu Shui (1/26)	**20** (1/27)
24 (2/02)	**25** (2/03)	**26** (2/04)	**27** (2/05)

Friday	Saturday	Sunday	Goals
	1 (lunar 1/08/20)	**2** (1/09)	
7 (1/14)	**8** (1/15)	**9** (1/16)	
14 (1/21)	**15** (1/22)	**16** (1/23)	
21 (1/28)	**22** (1/29)	**23** (lunar 2/01/20)	
28 (2/06)	**29** (2/07)		

March 2020

Monday	Tuesday	Wednesday	Thursday
2 (2/09)	**3** (2/10)	**4** (2/11)	**5** Jing Zhe (2/12)
9 (2/16)	**10** (2/17)	**11** (2/18)	**12** (2/19)
16 (2/23)	**17** (2/24)	**18** (2/25)	**19** (2/26)
23 (2/30)	**24** (lunar 3/01/20)	**25** (3/02)	**26** (3/03)
30 (3/07)	**31** (3/08)		

Friday	Saturday	Sunday	*Goals*
		1 (lunar 2/08/20)	
6 (2/13)	**7** (2/14)	**8** (2/15)	
13 (2/20)	**14** (2/21)	**15** (2/22)	
20 Chun Fen (2/27)	**21** (2/28)	**22** (2/29)	
27 (3/04)	**28** (3/05)	**29** (3/06)	

April 2020

Monday	Tuesday	Wednesday	Thursday
		1 (lunar 3/09/20)	**2** (3/10)
6 (3/14)	**7** (3/15)	**8** (3/16)	**9** (3/17)
13 (3/21)	**14** (3/22)	**15** (3/23)	**16** (3/24)
20 (3/28)	**21** (3/29)	**22** (3/30)	**23** (lunar 4/01/20)
27 (4/05)	**28** (4/06)	**29** (4/07)	**30** (4/08)

Friday	Saturday	Sunday	*Goals*
3 (3/11)	**4** Qing Ming (3/12)	**5** (3/13)	
10 (3/18)	**11** (3/19)	**12** (3/20)	
17 (3/25)	**18** (3/26)	**19** Gu Yu (3/27)	
24 (4/02)	**25** (4/03)	**26** (4/04)	

May 2020

Monday	Tuesday	Wednesday	Thursday
4 (4/12)	**5** Li Xia (4/13)	**6** (4/14)	**7** (4/15)
11 (4/19)	**12** (4/20)	**13** (4/21)	**14** (4/22)
18 (4/26)	**19** (4/27)	**20** Xiao Man (4/28)	**21** (4/29)
25 (4/03)	**26** (4/04)	**27** (4/05)	**28** (4/06)

Friday	Saturday	Sunday	*Goals*
1 (lunar 4/09/20)	**2** (4/10)	**3** (4/11)	
8 (4/16)	**9** (4/17)	**10** (4/18)	
15 (4/23)	**16** (4/24)	**17** (4/25)	
22 (4/30)	**23** (lunar leap April 4/01/20)	**24** (4/02)	
29 (4/07)	**30** (4/08)	**31** (4/09)	

May 2020

June 2020

Monday	Tuesday	Wednesday	Thursday
1 (lunar 4/10/20)	**2** (4/11)	**3** (4/12)	**4** (4/13)
8 (4/17)	**9** (4/18)	**10** (4/19)	**11** (4/20)
15 (4/24)	**16** (4/25)	**17** (4/26)	**18** (4/27)
22 (5/02)	**23** (5/03)	**24** (5/04)	**25** (5/05)
29 (5/09)	**30** (5/10)		

Friday	Saturday	Sunday	Goals
5 Mang Zhong (4/14)	**6** (4/15)	**7** (4/16)	
12 (4/21)	**13** (4/22)	**14** (4/23)	
19 (4/28)	**20** (4/29)	**21** Xia Zhi (lunar 5/01/20)	
26 (5/06)	**27** (5/07)	**28** (5/08)	

July 2020

Monday	Tuesday	Wednesday	Thursday
		1 (lunar 5/11/20)	**2** (5/12)
6 Xiao Shu (5/16)	**7** (5/17)	**8** (5/18)	**9** (5/19)
13 (5/23)	**14** (5/24)	**15** (5/25)	**16** (5/26)
20 (5/30)	**21** (lunar 6/01/20)	**22** Da Shu (6/02)	**23** (6/03)
27 (6/07)	**28** (6/08)	**29** (6/09)	**30** (6/10)

Friday	Saturday	Sunday	*Goals*
3 (5/13)	**4** (5/14)	**5** (5/15)	
10 (5/20)	**11** (5/21)	**12** (5/22)	
17 (5/27)	**18** (5/28)	**19** (5/29)	
24 (6/04)	**25** (6/05)	**26** (6/06)	
31 (6/11)			

August 2020

Monday	Tuesday	Wednesday	Thursday
3 (6/14)	**4** (6/15)	**5** (6/16)	**6** (6/17)
10 (6/21)	**11** (6/22)	**12** (6/23)	**13** (6/24)
17 (6/28)	**18** (6/29)	**19** (lunar 7/01/20)	**20** (7/02)
24 (7/06)	**25** (7/07)	**26** (7/08)	**27** (7/09)
31 (7/13)			

Friday	Saturday	Sunday	Goals
	1 (lunar 6/12/20)	**2** (6/13)	
7 Li Qiu (6/18)	**8** (6/19)	**9** (6/20)	
14 (6/25)	**15** (6/26)	**16** (6/27)	
21 (7/03)	**22** Chu Shu (7/04)	**23** (7/05)	
28 (7/10)	**29** (7/11)	**30** (7/12)	

September 2020

Monday	Tuesday	Wednesday	Thursday
	1 (lunar 7/14/20)	**2** (7/15)	**3** (7/16)
7 Bai Lu (7/20)	**8** (7/21)	**9** (7/22)	**10** (7/23)
14 (7/27)	**15** (7/28)	**16** (7/29)	**17** (lunar 8/01/20)
21 (8/05)	**22** Qiu Fen (8/06)	**23** (8/07)	**24** (8/08)
28 (8/12)	**29** (8/13)	**30** (8/14)	

Friday	Saturday	Sunday	Goals
4 (7/17)	**5** (7/18)	**6** (7/19)	
11 (7/24)	**12** (7/25)	**13** (7/26)	
18 (8/02)	**19** (8/03)	**20** (8/04)	
25 (8/09)	**26** (8/10)	**27** (8/11)	

October 2020

Monday	Tuesday	Wednesday	Thursday
			1 (lunar 8/15/20)
5 (8/19)	**6** (8/20)	**7** (8/21)	**8** Han Lu (8/22)
12 (8/26)	**13** (8/27)	**14** (8/28)	**15** (8/29)
19 (9/03)	**20** (9/04)	**21** (9/05)	**22** (9/06)
26 (9/10)	**27** (9/11)	**28** (9/12)	**29** (9/13)

Friday	Saturday	Sunday	*Goals*
2 (8/16)	**3** (8/17)	**4** (8/18)	
9 (8/23)	**10** (8/24)	**11** (8/25)	
16 (8/30)	**17** (lunar 9/01/20)	**18** (9/02)	
23 Shuang Jiang (9/07)	**24** (9/08)	**25** (9/09)	
30 (9/14)	**31** (9/15)		

October 2020

November 2020

Monday	Tuesday	Wednesday	Thursday
2 (9/17)	**3** (9/18)	**4** (9/19)	**5** (9/20)
9 (9/24)	**10** (9/25)	**11** (9/26)	**12** (9/27)
16 (10/02)	**17** (10/03)	**18** (10/04)	**19** (10/05)
23 (10/09)	**24** (10/10)	**25** (10/11)	**26** (10/12)
30 (10/16)			

Friday	Saturday	Sunday	*Goals*
		1 (lunar 9/16/20)	
6 (9/21)	**7** Li Dong (9/22)	**8** (9/23)	
13 (9/28)	**14** (9/29)	**15** (lunar 10/01/20)	
20 (10/6)	**21** (10/07)	**22** Xiao Xue (10/08)	
27 (10/13)	**28** (10/14)	**29** (10/15)	

November 2020

December 2020

Monday	Tuesday	Wednesday	Thursday
	1 (lunar 10/17/20)	**2** (10/18)	**3** (10/19)
7 Da Xue (10/23)	**8** (10/24)	**9** (10/25)	**10** (10/26)
14 (10/30)	**15** (lunar 11/01/20)	**16** (11/02)	**17** (11/03)
21 Dong Zhi (11/07)	**22** (11/08)	**23** (11/09)	**24** (11/10)
28 (11/14)	**29** (11/15)	**30** (11/16)	**31** (11/17)

Friday	Saturday	Sunday	Goals
4 (10/20)	**5** (10/21)	**6** (10/22)	
11 (10/27)	**12** (10/28)	**13** (10/29)	
18 (11/04)	**19** (11/05)	**20** (11/06)	
25 (11/11)	**26** (11/12)	**27** (11/13)	

January 2021

Monday	Tuesday	Wednesday	Thursday
4 (11/21)	**5** Xiao Han (11/22)	**6** (11/23)	**7** (11/24)
11 (11/28)	**12** (11/29)	**13** (lunar 12/01/20)	**14** (12/02)
18 (12/06)	**19** (12/07)	**20** Da Han (12/08)	**21** (12/09)
25 (12/13)	**26** (12/14)	**27** (12/15)	**28** (12/16)

Friday	Saturday	Sunday	Goals
1 (lunar 11/18/20)	**2** (11/19)	**3** (11/20)	
8 (11/25)	**9** (11/26)	**10** (11/27)	
15 (12/03)	**16** (12/04)	**17** (12/05)	
22 (12/10)	**23** (12/11)	**24** (12/12)	
29 (12/17)	**30** (12/18)	**31** (12/19)	

February 2021

Monday	Tuesday	Wednesday	Thursday
1 (lunar 12/20/20)	**2** (12/21)	**3** Li Chun (12/22)	**4** (12/23)
8 (12/27)	**9** (12/28)	**10** (12/29)	**11** (12/30)
15 (1/04/21)	**16** (1/05/21)	**17** (1/06/21)	**18** Yu Shui (1/07/21)
22 (1/11/21)	**23** (1/12/21)	**24** (1/13/21)	**25** (1/14/21)

Friday	Saturday	Sunday	Goals
5 (12/24)	**6** (12/25)	**7** (12/26)	
12 * Chinese New Year (lunar 1/01/21)	**13** (1/02/21)	**14** (1/03/21)	
19 (1/08/21)	**20** (1/09/21)	**21** (1/10/21)	
26 (1/15/21)	**27** (1/16/21)	**28** (1/17/21)	

January 2020 (Lunar calendar: 12/07/2019 to 1/07/2020)

	lucky directions	conflicting sign/direction	
Mon # 30 Earth	Southwest East	**Goat** **East**	*Favorable:* Wedding, meeting friends, religious ceremony, cleaning house. *Avoid:* Funeral.
Tue # 31 Metal	Southeast South	**Monkey** **North**	*Favorable:* Meeting friends, move the bed/furniture, starting business, trading, funeral, cremation. *Avoid:* Wedding, moving into a new house.
Wed # 1 Metal	Southeast South	**Rooster** **East**	*Favorable:* Fixing street/walkway. *Avoid:* **Any major festive event.** *** New Year's Day**
Thur # 2 Fire	Northeast Southeast	**Dog** **South**	*Favorable:* Wedding, ceremony, travel, starting construction, dress making, activating a statue, moving to a new house, setting up a bed, funeral. *Avoid:* Starting a business, setting up kitchen stove.
Fri # 3 Fire	Northwest Southeast	**Pig** **East**	*Favorable:* Ceremony, meeting friends, bathing, haircut, renovation, starting a construction, setting up a bed/stove, moving to a new house. *Avoid:* Wedding.
Sat # 4 Water	Southwest West	**Rat** **North**	*Favorable:* Visiting a doctor, demolition of a house. *Avoid:* **Any major festive event.**
Sun # 5 Water	South West	**Ox** **West**	*Favorable:* Religious blessing and ceremony, travel, activating a statue, wedding, renovation, setting up a bed, starting construction, hunting, funeral. *Avoid:* Starting a business, moving into a new house.

January 2020

Goals & Plans

Mon **30** Earth	
Tue **31** Metal	
Wed **1** Metal	
Thur **2** Fire	
Fri **3** Fire	
Sat **4** Water	
Sun **5** Water	

January 2020

	lucky directions	conflicting sign/direction	
Mon **6** Earth	Southeast North	**Tiger** **South**	*Favorable:* Travel, setting up a stove, moving to a new house, funeral, ceremony, starting a business. *Avoid:* Wedding.
Tue **7** Earth	Northeast North	**Rabbit** **East**	*Favorable:* Ceremony, bathing, pest control, removing Feng Shui cures. *Avoid:* **Any major festive event.**
Wed **8** Metal	Northwest East	**Dragon** **North**	*Favorable:* Wedding, meeting friends, trading, setting up a stove, ceremony, hunting. *Avoid:* Funeral, starting a business.
Thur **9** Metal	Southwest East	**Snake** **West**	*Favorable:* Starting a construction, dress making, setting up a bed/door/stove, starting a business, trading, adopting animals. *Avoid:* Funeral, wedding.
Fri **10** Wood	South	**Horse** **South**	*Favorable:* Ceremony, bathing, setting up a bed, trading, funeral. *Avoid:* Starting a business or construction.
Sat **11** Wood	Southeast South	**Goat** **East**	*Favorable:* Ceremony, removing Feng Shui cures. *Avoid:* **Any major festive event.**
Sun **12** Water	Northeast Southeast	**Monkey** **North**	*Favorable:* Wedding, dress making, starting a construction, renovation, setting up a bed/door, funeral, starting a business. *Avoid:* Visiting sick patients, travel.

January 2020

Goals & Plans

Mon **6** Earth	
Tue **7** Earth	
Wed **8** Metal	
Thur **9** Metal	
Fri **10** Wood	
Sat **11** Wood	
Sun **12** Water	

January 2020

	lucky directions	conflicting sign/direction	
Mon **13** Water	Northwest Southeast	**Rooster** **West**	*Favorable:* Wedding, dress making, ceremony, travel, starting a business, trading, setting up a bed, funeral. *Avoid:* Moving to a new house, starting a construction.
Tue **14** Earth	Southwest West	**Dog** **South**	*Favorable:* Ceremony, wedding, dress making, meeting friends, trading, fixing street/walkway. *Avoid:* Funeral, setting up a stove.
Wed **15** Earth	South West	**Pig** **East**	*Favorable:* Ceremony. *Avoid:* **Any major festive event.**
Thur **16** Fire	Southeast North	**Rat** **North**	*Favorable:* Travel, wedding, dress making, setting up a bed, funeral, ceremony, bathing, haircut, pest control, hunting. *Avoid:* Starting a business, setting up a stove.
Fri **17** Fire	Northeast North	**Ox** **West**	*Favorable:* Ceremony, bathing, demolition of a house. *Avoid:* **Any major festive event.**
Sat **18** Wood	Northwest East	**Tiger** **South**	*Favorable:* Ceremony, travel, dress making, moving to a new house, setting up a stove/door, funeral, starting a business. *Avoid:* Setting up a bed.
Sun **19** Wood	Southwest East	**Rabbit** **East**	*Favorable:* Ceremony, removing Feng Shui cures, funeral. *Avoid:* **Any major festive event.**

5

January 2020

Goals and Plans

Mon **13** Water	
Tue **14** Earth	
Wed **15** Earth	
Thur **16** Fire	
Fri **17** Fire	
Sat **18** Wood	
Sun **19** Wood	

January 2020

	lucky directions	conflicting sign/direction	
Mon **20** Water	South	**Dragon** **North**	*Favorable:* Hunting, ceremony. *Avoid:* Starting a business, setting up a bed.
Tue **21** Water	Southeast South	**Snake** **West**	*Favorable:* Meeting friends, haircut, ceremony, setting up a stove. *Avoid:* Funeral, wedding, travel.
Wed **22** Metal	Northeast Southeast	**Horse** **South**	*Favorable:* Ceremony, dress making, funeral, setting up a bed/door, trading. *Avoid:* Wedding, moving to a new house.
Thur **23** Metal	Northwest Southeast	**Goat** **East**	*Favorable:* Ceremony, removing Feng Shui cures. *Avoid:* **Any major festive event.**
Fri **24** Fire	Southwest West	**Monkey** **North**	*Favorable:* Wedding, dress making, trading, setting up a bed, moving to a new house, funeral. *Avoid:* Ceremony, starting a construction.
Sat **25** Fire	South West	**Rooster** **West**	*Favorable:* Ceremony, travel, setting up a bed, starting a business, trading, funeral. *Avoid:* Setting up a stove, wedding.　　***Lunar New Year**
Sun **26** Wood	Southeast North	**Dog** **South**	*Favorable:* Ceremony, fixing street/walkway or walls. *Avoid:* Wedding, moving to a new house.

January 2020

Goals & Plans

Mon **20** Water	
Tue **21** Water	
Wed **22** Metal	
Thur **23** Metal	
Fri **24** Fire	
Sat **25** Fire	
Sun **26** Wood	

January - February 2020

	lucky directions	conflicting sign/direction	
Mon **27** Wood	Northeast North	Pig East	*Favorable:* Construction, ceremony, wedding, dress making, setting up a bed or stove, moving to a new house. *Avoid:* funeral.
Tue **28** Earth	Northwest East	Rat North	*Favorable:* Wedding, ceremony, bathing, haircut, travel, funeral. *Avoid:* Starting a construction or business, moving to a new house.
Wed **29** Earth	Southwest East	Ox West	*Favorable:* Ceremony, demolition of a house, removing Feng Shui cures. *Avoid:* **Any major festive event.**
Thur **30** Metal	South	Tiger South	*Favorable:* Starting a business, ceremony, haircut, activating a Feng Shui cure, travel, wedding, trading, funeral. *Avoid:* Moving to a new house, setting up a bed.
Fri **31** Metal	Southeast South	Rabbit East	*Favorable:* Ceremony, funeral, removing Feng Shui cures. *Avoid:* **Any major festive event.**
Sat **1** Fire	Northeast Southeast	Dragon North	*Favorable:* Ceremony, hunting, wedding, dress making, setting up a stove. *Avoid:* Setting up a bed, starting a business.
Sun **2** Fire	Northwest Southeast	Snake West	*Favorable:* Ceremony, starting a business, removing Feng Shui cures, haircut, dress making, moving to a new house, setting up a bed or stove. *Avoid:* Wedding, funeral.

January - February 2020

Goals & Plans

Mon **27** Wood	
Tue **28** Earth	
Wed **29** Earth	
Thur **30** Metal	
Fri **31** Metal	
Sat **1** Fire	
Sun **2** Fire	

February 2020   (Lunar calendar: 1/08 to 2/07/2020)

	lucky directions	conflicting sign/direction	
Mon **3** Water	Southwest West	**Horse** **South**	*Favorable:* Ceremony, bathing, funeral, trading, *Avoid:* Wedding, setting up a stove.
Tue **4** Water	South West	**Goat** **East**	*Favorable:* Ceremony, funeral. *** Starting of Spring (Li Chun)** *Avoid:* Wedding, starting a construction.
Wed **5** Earth	Southeast North	**Monkey** **North**	*Favorable:* Wedding, dress making, meeting friends, trading, funeral, activating a statue, removing Feng Shui cures, adopting animals, setting up a bed. *Avoid:* Moving to a new house, starting a construction.
Thur **6** Earth	Northeast North	**Rooster** **West**	*Favorable:* Wedding, dress making, travel, starting a construction, ceremony, setting up a bed/door, starting a business, planting, funeral. *Avoid:* Moving to a new house, setting up a stove.
Fri **7** Metal	Northwest East	**Dog** **South**	*Favorable:* Meeting friends, ceremony, pest countrol. *Avoid:* Starting a business, starting a construction, funeral.
Sat **8** Metal	Southwest East	**Pig** **East**	*Favorable:* Ceremony, fixing street/walkway. *Avoid:* Funeral, wedding.
Sun **9** Wood	South	**Rat** **North**	*Favorable:* Wedding, dress making, travel, starting a construction, startingma business, trading, planting, funeral, ceremony, activating a statue, moving to a new house. *Avoid:* Visiting sick patients, setting up a stove.

February 2020

Goals & Plans

Mon **3** Water	
Tue **4** Water	
Wed **5** Earth	
Thur **6** Earth	
Fri **7** Metal	
Sat **8** Metal	
Sun **9** Wood	

February 2020

	lucky directions	conflicting sign/direction	
Mon **10** Wood	Southeast South	**Ox** **West**	*Favorable:* Meeting friends, wedding, travel, ceremony. *Avoid:* Moving to a new house, starting a construction.
Tue **11** Water	Northeast Southeast	**Tiger** **South**	*Favorable:* Ceremony, bathing, cleaning house, demolition of a house. *Avoid:* **Any major festive event.**
Wed **12** Water	Northwest Southeast	**Rabbit** **East**	*Favorable:* Funeral, ceremony, travel, wedding, dress making, starting a construction, moving to a new house, starting a business, trading. *Avoid:* Setting up a bed or stove.
Thur **13** Earth	Southwest West	**Dragon** **North**	*Favorable:* Ceremony, removing Feng Shui cures, funeral. *Avoid:* **Any major festive event.**
Fri **14** Earth	South West	**Snake** **West**	*Favorable:* Wedding, meeting friends, travel, starting a construction, planting, ceremony, activating a statue, setting up a bed. *Avoid:* Funeral, moving to a new house.
Sat **15** Fire	Southeast North	**Horse** **South**	*Favorable:* Ceremony, travel, wedding, starting a construction, haircut, dress making, starting a business, trading, *Avoid:* Funeral, moving to a new house.
Sun **16** Fire	Northeast North	**Goat** **East**	*Favorable:* Ceremony, pest control, setting up a bed/stove, funeral. *Avoid:* Wedding, moving to a new house, travel.

February 2020

Goals & Plans

Mon **10** Wood	
Tue **11** Water	
Wed **12** Water	
Thur **13** Earth	
Fri **14** Earth	
Sat **15** Fire	
Sun **16** Fire	

February 2020

Mon **17** Wood	Northwest East	Monkey North	*Favorable:* Meeting friends, trading, dress making, adopting animals, funeral. *Avoid:* Wedding, moving to a new house.
Tue **18** Wood	Southwest East	Rooster West	*Favorable:* Ceremony, travel, meeting friends, funeral, starting a construction, trading, starting a business, setting up a door/bed, dress making. *Avoid:* Wedding, moving to a new house.
Wed **19** Water	South	Dog South	*Favorable:* Wedding, meeting friends, travel, trading, removing Feng Shui cures, adopting animals. *Avoid:* Funeral.
Thur **20** Water	Southeast South	Pig East	*Favorable:* Fixing steet/walkway, setting up a stove. *Avoid:* Funeral, ceremony.
Fri **21** Metal	Northeast Southeast	Rat North	*Favorable:* Ceremony, wedding, dress making, travel, starting a construction, starting a business, trading, moving to a new house, setting up a bed/door. *Avoid:* Funeral.
Sat **22** Metal	Northwest Southeast	Ox West	*Favorable:* Wedding, dress making, ceremony, hunting, fishing, ceremony, funeral. *Avoid:* Starting a business, starting a construction.
Sun **23** Fire	Southwest West	Tiger South	*Favorable:* Ceremony, bathing, removing Feng Shui cures, house cleaning and demolition. *Avoid:* **Any major festive event.**

February 2020

Goals & Plans

Mon **17** Wood	
Tue **18** Wood	
Wed **19** Water	
Thur **20** Water	
Fri **21** Metal	
Sat **22** Metal	
Sun **23** Fire	

February - March 2020

	lucky directions	conflicting sign/direction	
Mon **24** Fire	South West	**Rabbit** **East**	*Favorable:* Wedding, travel, starting a construction, starting a business, funeral, ceremony, moving to a new house, dress making. *Avoid:* Setting up a bed or stove.
Tue **25** Wood	Southeast North	**Dragon** **North**	*Favorable:* Pest control, hunting, fishing, funeral. *Avoid:* **Any major festive event.**
Wed **26** Wood	Northeast North	**Snake** **West**	*Favorable:* Ceremony, bathing, haircut, wedding, meeting friends, planting, fishing, setting up a bed. *Avoid:* Funeral, setting up a stove.
Thur **27** Earth	Northwest East	**Horse** **South**	*Favorable:* Ceremony, bathing, haircut, travel, wedding, starting a business, trading. *Avoid:* Funeral, moving to a new house.
Fri **28** Earth	Southwest East	**Goat** **East**	*Favorable:* Ceremony, funeral. *Avoid:* Moving to a new house, setting up a stove, wedding, travel, starting a construction.
Sat **29** Metal	South	**Monkey** **North**	*Favorable:* Meeting freinds, starting a business, trading, funeral, removing Feng Shui cures, adopting animals, setting up a bed, dress making. *Avoid:* Wedding, moving to a new house.
Sun **1** Metal	Southeast South	**Rooster** **West**	*Favorable:* Travel, trading, starting a business, ceremony, wedding, moving to a new house, setting up a bed, funeral. *Avoid:* Setting up a stove.

February - March 2020

Mon **24** Fire	
Tue **25** Wood	
Wed **26** Wood	
Thur **27** Earth	
Fri **28** Earth	
Sat **29** Metal	
Sun **1** Metal	

March 2020 (Lunar calendar: 2/08 to 3/08/2020)

	lucky directions	conflicting sign/direction	
Mon **2** Fire	Northeast Southeast	Dog South	*Favorable:* Meeting friends, ceremony, setting up a bed, activating a statue. *Avoid:* Funeral, wedding.
Tue **3** Fire	Northwest Southeast	Pig East	*Favorable:* Setting up a stove, fixing up street/walkway, removing Feng Shui cures. *Avoid:* Funeral, travel.
Wed **4** Water	Southwest West	Rat North	*Favorable:* Wedding, dress making, travel, renovation, starting a construction, starting a business, activating a statue, funeral, setting up a bed. *Avoid:* Setting up a stove, ceremony.
Thur **5** Water	South West	Ox West	*Favorable:* Travel, starting a construction, funeral, wedding, setting up a bed, moving to a new house. *Avoid:* none.
Fri **6** Earth	Southeast North	Tiger South	*Favorable:* Travel, dress making, activating a statue, starting a construction, moving to a new house, ceremony, funeral, cremation. *Avoid:* Starting a business, setting up a bed.
Sat **7** Earth	Northeast North	Rabbit East	*Favorable:* Demolition of a house. *Avoid:* **Any major festive event.**
Sun **8** Metal	Northwest East	Dragon North	*Favorable:* Travel, meeting friends, starting a construction, setting up a bed/door/stove, funeral, cremation. *Avoid:* Wedding.

March 2020

Goals & Plans

Mon **2** Fire	
Tue **3** Fire	
Wed **4** Water	
Thur **5** Water	
Fri **6** Earth	
Sat **7** Earth	
Sun **8** Metal	

March 2020

	lucky directions	conflicting sign/direction	
Mon **9** Metal	Southwest East	**Snake** **West**	*Favorable:* Meeting friends, travel, starting a construction, starting a business, trading, dress making, activating a statue, moving to a new house, setting up a bed/door/stove. *Avoid:* Wedding, funeral.
Tue **10** Wood	South	**Horse** **South**	*Favorable:* Haircut, planting, hunting. *Avoid:* Starting a business, wedding.
Wed **11** Wood	Southeast South	**Goat** **East**	*Favorable:* Meeting friends, travel, wedding, moving to a new house, setting a bed/door/stove, ceremony, dress making, haircut. *Avoid:* Funeral, starting a business.
Thur **12** Water	Northeast Southeast	**Monkey** **North**	*Favorable:* Starting a construction, funeral, setting up a bed or stove. *Avoid:* Starting a business, wedding.
Fri **13** Water	Northwest Southeast	**Rooster** **West**	*Favorable:* Ceremony, meeting friends, travel, starting a business, trading, setting up a bed, dress making. *Avoid:* Funeral, visiting sick patients.
Sat **14** Earth	Southwest West	**Dog** **South**	*Favorable:* Ceremony, removing Feng Shui cures, house cleaning, travel, hunting. *Avoid:* **Any major festive event.**
Sun **15** Earth	South West	**Pig** **East**	*Favorable:* Wedding, meeting friends, starting a business, trading, removing Feng Shui cures, ceremony. *Avoid:* Moving to a new house, funeral.

March 2020

Goals & Plans

Mon **9** Metal	
Tue **10** Wood	
Wed **11** Wood	
Thur **12** Water	
Fri **13** Water	
Sat **14** Earth	
Sun **15** Earth	

March 2020

	lucky directions	conflicting sign/direction	
Mon **16** Fire	Southeast North	**Rat** **North**	*Favorable:* Ceremony, fixing street/walkway/wall. *Avoid:* Moving to a new house, wedding.
Tue **17** Fire	Northeast North	**Ox** **West**	*Favorable:* Ceremony, travel, starting a construction, starting a business, funeral, wedding, moving to a new house, activating a statue, setting up a bed/door/stove. *Avoid:* none.
Wed **18** Wood	Northwest East	**Tiger** **South**	*Favorable:* Cleaning the house, bathing, ceremony, removing Feng Shui cures, funeral. *Avoid:* Moving to a new house, wedding.
Thur **19** Wood	Southwest East	**Rabbit** **East**	*Favorable:* House demolition. *Avoid:* Any major festive event.
Fri **20** Water	South	**Dragon** **North**	*Favorable:* Starting a construction, starting a business, dress making, trading, hunting, fishing, funeral. *Avoid:* Travel, wedding.
Sat **21** Water	Southeast South	**Snake** **West**	*Favorable:* Visiting a doctor, ceremony, starting a construction, moving to a new house, setting up a bed/stove, starting a business, trading, dress making. *Avoid:* Funeral.
Sun **22** Metal	Northeast Southeast	**Horse** **South**	*Favorable:* Ceremony, haircut, wedding, pest control. *Avoid:* Moving to a new house, funeral.

March 2020

Goals & Plans

Mon **16** Fire	
Tue **17** Fire	
Wed **18** Wood	
Thur **19** Wood	
Fri **20** Water	
Sat **21** Water	
Sun **22** Metal	

March 2020

	lucky directions	conflicting sign/direction	
Mon **23** Metal	Northwest Southeast	**Goat East**	*Favorable:* Meeting friends, wedding, dress making, ceremony, travel, renovation, starting a construction, moving to a new house, setting up a bed/door/stove. *Avoid:* Funeral.
Tue **24** Fire	Southwest West	**Monkey North**	*Favorable:* Funeral, planting, haircut, starting a construction, setting up a bed/door. *Avoid:* Moving to a new house.
Wed **25** Fire	South West	**Rooster West**	*Favorable:* Ceremony, travel, starting a business, trading, wedding, dress making, funeral, moving to a new house, visiting a doctor. *Avoid:* Setting up a stove.
Thur **26** Wood	Southeast North	**Dog South**	*Favorable:* Travel, bathing, haircut, cleaning houses. *Avoid:* **Any major festive event.**
Fri **27** Wood	Northeast North	**Pig East**	*Favorable:* Meeting friends, trading, ceremony, haircut, setting up a bed/door/stove, removing Feng Shui cures, activating a statue, dress making. *Avoid:* Wedding, moving to a new house.
Sat **28** Earth	Northwest East	**Rat North**	*Favorable:* Ceremony, fixing street/walkway, wedding. *Avoid:* Visiting sick patients, setting up a stove.
Sun **29** Earth	Southwest East	**Ox West**	*Favorable:* Wedding, dress making, starting a business, trading, travel, ceremony, moving to a new house, setting up a bed, funeral. *Avoid:* none.

March 2020

Goals & Plans

Mon **23** Metal	
Tue **24** Fire	
Wed **25** Fire	
Thur **26** Wood	
Fri **27** Wood	
Sat **28** Earth	
Sun **29** Earth	

March - April 2020

	lucky directions	conflicting sign/direction	
Mon **30** Metal	South	**Tiger** **South**	*Favorable:* Ceremony, bathing, dress making, starting a construction, moving to a new house, setting up a door, haircut, funeral, cremation. *Avoid:* none.
Tue **31** Metal	Southeast South	**Rabbit** **East**	*Favorable:* House demolition, visiting a doctor. *Avoid:* **Any major festive event.**
Wed **1** Fire	Northeast Southeast	**Dragon** **North**	*Favorable:* Travel, starting a construction, starting a business, trading, funeral, setting up a bed/stove, ceremony, dress making. *Avoid:* Wedding.
Thur **2** Fire	Northwest Southeast	**Snake** **West**	*Favorable:* Travel, dress making, starting a construction, signing contract, moving to a new house, setting up a bed/stove, starting a business, trading. *Avoid:* Wedding, Funeral.
Fri **3** Water	Southeast South	**Horse** **South**	*Favorable:* Wedding, dress making, setting up a bed, hunting, planting. *Avoid:* Starting a business, funeral.
Sat **4** Water	South West	**Goat** **East**	*Favorable:* Ceremony, wedding, travel, planting, starting a construction, removing a Feng Shui cure, moving to a new house. *Avoid:* none.
Sun **5** Earth	Southeast North	**Monkey** **North**	*Favorable:* Wedding, travel, dress making, starting a construction, starting a business, trading, moving to a new house, setting up a bed/stove, planting. *Avoid:* Funeral.

March - April 2020

Goals & Plans

Mon **30** Metal	
Tue **31** Metal	
Wed **1** Fire	
Thur **2** Fire	
Fri **3** Water	
Sat **4** Water	
Sun **5** Earth	

April 2020   (Lunar calendar: 3/09 to 4/08/2020)

	lucky directions	conflicting sign/direction	
Mon **6** Earth	Northeast North	**Rooster** **West**	*Favorable:* Ceremony, wedding, dress making, setting up a bed/stove, trading, funeral. *Avoid:* Visiting sick patients.
Tue **7** Metal	Northwest East	**Dog** **South**	*Favorable:* Ceremony, starting a business, travel, removing Feng Shui cures. *Avoid:* Funeral.
Wed **8** Metal	Southwest East	**Pig** **East**	*Favorable:* House cleaning, activating a statue, haircut, wedding, meeting friends, planting. *Avoid:* Moving to a new house, trading.
Thur **9** Wood	South	**Rat** **North**	*Favorable:* Ceremony, travel, starting a business, trading, setting up a bed, dress making, activating a statue. *Avoid:* Wedding, funeral.
Fri **10** Wood	Southeast South	**Ox** **West**	*Favorable:* Ceremony, starting a business, setting up a stove, fixing a street and walkway. *Avoid:* Funeral, setting up a bed.
Sat **11** Water	Northeast Southeast	**Tiger** **South**	*Favorable:* Ceremony, activating a statue, dress making, starting a construction, starting a business, trading, funeral. *Avoid:* Wedding, setting up a bed.
Sun **12** Water	Northwest Southeast	**Rabbit** **East**	*Favorable:* Ceremony, wedding, dress making, travel, visiting a doctor, activating a statue, funeral, moving to a new house, setting up a bed/stove. *Avoid:* Planting, starting a construction.

April 2020

Goals & Plans

Mon **6** Earth	
Tue **7** Metal	
Wed **8** Metal	
Thur **9** Wood	
Fri **10** Wood	
Sat **11** Water	
Sun **12** Water	

April 2020

	lucky directions	conflicting sign/direction	
Mon **13** Earth	Southwest West	Dragon North	*Favorable:* Ceremony, bathing, house demolition, removing Feng Shui cures. *Avoid:* **Any major festive event.**
Tue **14** Earth	South West	Snake West	*Favorable:* Ceremony, bathing, hunting, fishing. *Avoid:* **Any major festive event.**
Wed **15** Fire	Southeast North	Horse South	*Favorable:* Ceremony, travel, starting a construction, starting a business, trading, dress making, planting, setting up a bed/stove. *Avoid:* Funeral, starting a business.
Thur **16** Fire	Northeast North	Goat East	*Favorable:* Ceremony, fishing, hunting. *Avoid:* **Any major festive event.**
Fri **17** Wood	Northwest East	Monkey North	*Favorable:* Wedding, meeting friends, travel, starting a business, trading, starting a construction, dress making, activating a statue. *Avoid:* Moving to a new house, setting up a bed.
Sat **18** Wood	Southwest East	Rooster West	*Favorable:* Ceremony, wedding, setting up a bed/stove, funeral. *Avoid:* Setting up a door.
Sun **19** Water	South	Dog South	*Favorable:* Travel, wedding, setting up a bed, starting a business, trading. *Avoid:* Funeral, activating a statue.

31

April 2020

Goals & Plans

Mon **13** Earth	
Tue **14** Earth	
Wed **15** Fire	
Thur **16** Fire	
Fri **17** Wood	
Sat **18** Wood	
Sun **19** Water	

April 2020

	lucky directions	conflicting sign/direction	
Mon **20** Water	Southeast South	Pig East	*Favorable:* Wedding, haircut, bathing, meeting friends, moving to a new house, setting up a bed/stove, dress making, activating a statue. *Avoid:* Funeral, starting a business.
Tue **21** Metal	Northeast Southeast	Rat North	*Favorable:* Ceremony, haircut, wedding, setting up a bed, meeting friends, starting a business, funeral. *Avoid:* Moving to a new house, starting a construction.
Wed **22** Metal	Northwest Southeast	Ox West	*Favorable:* Ceremony, starting a business, setting up a stove. *Avoid:* Funeral, planting.
Thur **23** Fire	Southwest West	Tiger South	*Favorable:* Ceremony, activating a statue, dress making, starting a business, funeral. *Avoid:* Wedding, moving to a new house.
Fri **24** Fire	South West	Rabbit East	*Favorable:* Ceremony, wedding, dress making, trading, funeral, setting up a bed/door, travel, visiting a doctor. *Avoid:* Moving to a new house.
Sat **25** Wood	Southeast North	Dragon North	*Favorable:* Ceremony, bathing, house demolition, removing Feng Shui cures. *Avoid:* **Any major festive event.**
Sun **26** Wood	Northeast North	Snake West	*Favorable:* Bathing, fishing. *Avoid:* **Any major festive event.**

April 2020

Goals & Plans

Mon **20** Water	
Tue **21** Metal	
Wed **22** Metal	
Thur **23** Fire	
Fri **24** Fire	
Sat **25** Wood	
Sun **26** Wood	

April - May 2020

	lucky directions	conflicting sign/direction	
Mon **27** Earth	Northwest East	**Horse** **South**	*Favorable:* Meeting friends, wedding, ceremony, trading, funeral, setting up bed/door, dress making, activating a statue. *Avoid:* Starting a business, travel.
Tue **28** Earth	Southwest East	**Goat** **East**	*Favorable:* Ceremony, house cleaning, pest control, fishing. *Avoid:* Any major festive event.
Wed **29** Metal	South	**Monkey** **North**	*Favorable:* Meeting friends, travel, starting a business, trading, setting up a bed, dress making. *Avoid:* Moving to a new house, wedding, visiting patients.
Thur **30** Metal	Southeast South	**Rooster** **West**	*Favorable:* Travel, wedding, dress making, trading, pest control, setting up a bed/stove, funeral. *Avoid:* Starting a business.
Fri **1** Fire	Northeast Southeast	**Dog** **South**	*Favorable:* Travel, training animals (horse/cow). *Avoid:* **Any major festive event.**
Sat **2** Fire	Northwest Southeast	**Pig** **East**	*Favorable:* Ceremony, bathing, haircut, wedding, moving to a new house, setting up a bed, dress making. *Avoid:* Starting a business, setting up a stove.
Sun **3** Water	Southwest West	**Rat** **North**	*Favorable:* Ceremony, travel, haircut, wedding, meeting friends, setting up a bed, starting a business, funeral, activating a statue. *Avoid:* Setting up a stove/door, moving to a new house.

April - May 2020

Goals & Plans

Mon **27** Earth	
Tue **28** Earth	
Wed **29** Metal	
Thur **30** Metal	
Fri **1** Fire	
Sat **2** Fire	
Sun **3** Water	

May 2020 (Lunar calendar: 4/09 to *leap month* 4/09/2020)

	lucky directions	conflicting sign/direction	
Mon **4** Water	South West	**Ox** **West**	*Favorable:* Ceremony, fixing street/walkway/wall, removing Feng Shui cures. *Avoid:* **Any major festive event.**
Tue **5** Earth	Southeast North	**Tiger** **South**	*Favorable:* Ceremony, activating a statue, house cleaning, fixing street/walkway. *Avoid:* Wedding, moving to a new house.
Wed **6** Earth	Northeast North	**Rabbit** **East**	*Favorable:* Ceremony, travel, bathing, hiarcut, starting a business, trading, funeral, moving to a new house, setting up bed/stove, renovation, dress making. *Avoid:* Wedding.
Thur **7** Metal	Northwest East	**Dragon** **North**	*Favorable:* Ceremony, wedding, meeting friends, haircut, starting a construction, planting, funeral. *Avoid:* Moving to a new house.
Fri **8** Metal	Southwest East	**Snake** **West**	*Favorable:* Ceremony, bathing, house demolition, removing Feng Shui cures. *Avoid:* **Avoid any major festive event.**
Sat **9** Wood	South	**Horse** **South**	*Favorable:* House cleaning, bathing. *Avoid:* Wedding, starting a business.
Sun **10** Wood	Southwest South	**Goat** **East**	*Favorable:* Meeting friends, travel, starting a construction, starting a business, trading, setting up a bed/stove, planting, funeral, dress making. *Avoid:* Wedding.

May 2020

Goals & Plans

Mon **4** Water	
Tue **5** Earth	
Wed **6** Earth	
Thur **7** Metal	
Fri **8** Metal	
Sat **9** Wood	
Sun **10** Wood	

May 2020

	lucky directions	conflicting sign/direction	
Mon **11** Water	Northeast Southeast	Monkey North	*Favorable:* Planting, hunting, pest control. *Avoid:* Visiting sick patients, starting a business/construction, funeral.
Tue **12** Water	Northwest Southeast	Rooster West	*Favorable:* Wedding, ceremony, starting a construction, starting a business, trading, setting up a bed, dress making, activating a statue. *Avoid:* Funeral, moving to a new house.
Wed **13** Earth	Southwest West	Dog South	*Favorable:* Ceremony, wedding, dress making, moving to a new house, setting up a bed, trading, house cleaning. *Avoid:* Funeral, setting up a stove.
Thur **14** Earth	South West	Pig East	*Favorable:* Meeting friends, pest control. *Avoid:* **Any major festive event.**
Fri **15** Fire	Southeast North	Rat North	*Favorable:* Ceremony, travel, wedding, dress making, renovation, moving to a new house, planting, funeral. *Avoid:* Starting a construction.
Sat **16** Fire	East North	Ox West	*Favorable:* Ceremony, pest control. *Avoid:* **Any major festive event.**
Sun **17** Wood	Northwest East	Tiger South	*Favorable:* Ceremony, wedding, meeting friends, travel, starting a construction, planting, funeral, activating a statue. *Avoid:* Starting a business, wedding.

May 2020

Goals & Plans

Mon **11** Water	
Tue **12** Water	
Wed **13** Earth	
Thur **14** Earth	
Fri **15** Fire	
Sat **16** Fire	
Sun **17** Wood	

May 2020

	lucky directions	conflicting sign/direction	
Mon **18** Wood	Southeast East	**Rabbit** **East**	*Favorable:* Ceremony, wedding, travel, haircut, starting a construction, starting a business, funeral, moving to a new house, setting up a bed/stove, dress making. *Avoid:* Setting up a door, activating a statue.
Tue **19** Water	South	**Dragon** **North**	*Favorable:* Bathing, haircut, wedding, starting a construction, setting up a door/bed, funeral, dress making, activating a statue. *Avoid:* Starting a business.
Wed **20** Water	Southeast South	**Snake** **West**	*Favorable:* House demolition. *Avoid:* **Any major festive event.**
Thur **21** Metal	Northeast Southeast	**Horse** **South**	*Favorable:* Ceremony, travel, wedding, renovation, starting a construction, moving to a new house, setting up a door/bed/stove, funeral, dress making, activating a statue. *Avoid:* none.
Fri **22** Metal	Northwest Southeast	**Goat** **East**	*Favorable:* none *Avoid:* **Any major festive event.**
Sat **23** Fire	Southwest West	**Monkey** **North**	*Favorable:* Wedding, meeting friends, travel, starting a business, trading, adopting animals, removing Feng Shui cures, dress making. *Avoid:* Funeral.
Sun **24** Fire	South West	**Rooster** **West**	*Favorable:* Ceremony, travel, wedding, starting a construction, trading, planting, funeral, activating a statue, dress making. *Avoid:* Moving to a new house.

May 2020

Goals & Plans

Mon **18** Wood	
Tue **19** Water	
Wed **20** Water	
Thur **21** Metal	
Fri **22** Metal	
Sat **23** Fire	
Sun **24** Fire	

May 2020

	lucky directions	conflicting sign/direction	
Mon **25** Wood	Southeast North	**Dog** **South**	*Favorable:* Ceremony, travel, wedding, moving to a new house, setting up a bed/stove, trading, funeral, dress making. *Avoid:* Adopting animals.
Tue **26** Wood	Northeast North	**Pig** **East**	*Favorable:* Pest control. *Avoid:* **Any major festive event.**
Wed **27** Earth	Northwest East	**Rat** **North**	*Favorable:* Ceremony, wedding, moving, starting a construction, funeral, trading, dress making, activating a statue. *Avoid:* Starting a business.
Thur **28** Earth	Southwest East	**Ox** **West**	*Favorable:* Ceremony, bathing, house cleaning, fixing street/walkway, wedding, setting up a bed/stove. *Avoid:* Starting a business, funeral.
Fri **29** Metal	South	**Tiger** **South**	*Favorable:* Ceremony, bathing, house cleaning, fixing street/walkway, funeral. *Avoid:* Wedding, moving to a new house, travel.
Sat **30** Metal	Southeast South	**Rabbit** **East**	*Favorable:* Wedding, travel, starting a construction, starting a business, trading, moving to a new house, setting up a stove/bed, dress making, activating a statue, ceremony. *Avoid:* none.
Sun **31** Fire	Northeast Southeast	**Dragon** **North**	*Favorable:* Ceremony, haircut, travel, wedding, meeting friends, starting a construction, funeral. *Avoid:* Moving to a new house, wedding.

May 2020

Goals & Plans

Mon **25** Wood	
Tue **26** Wood	
Wed **27** Earth	
Thur **28** Earth	
Fri **29** Metal	
Sat **30** Metal	
Sun **31** Fire	

June 2020 (Lunar calendar: *leap month* 4/10 to 5/10/2020)

	lucky directions	conflicting sign/direction	
Mon **1** Fire	Northwest Southeast	**Snake** **West**	*Favorable:* Ceremony, bathing, house demolition, removing Feng Shui cures. *Avoid:* **Any major festive event.**
Tue **2** Water	Southeast East	**Horse** **South**	*Favorable:* Ceremony, meeting friends, travel, starting a construction, starting a business, trading, planting, wedding, moving to a new house, setting up a bed/door, dress making. *Avoid:* Funeral.
Wed **3** Water	South West	**Goat** **East**	*Favorable:* Starting a construction, starting a business, trading, funeral, setting up a door/bed, visiting a doctor, activating a statue. *Avoid:* Moving to a new house, wedding.
Thur **4** Earth	Southeast North	**Monkey** **North**	*Favorable:* Hunting, fishing. *Avoid:* **Any major festive event.**
Fri **5** Earth	Northeast North	**Rooster** **West**	*Favorable:* Wedding, travel, setting up a bed/stove, starting a business, ceremony, activating a statue. *Avoid:* Funeral, visiting sick patients.
Sat **6** Metal	Northwest East	**Dog** **South**	*Favorable:* Ceremony, bathing, haircut, house cleaning, fixing street/walkway. *Avoid:* **Any major festive event.**
Sun **7** Metal	Southwest East	**Pig** **East**	*Favorable:* Ceremony, planting, adopting animals, wedding, starting a construction, moving to a new house, setting up a door/bed, dress making. *Avoid:* Funeral, setting up a bed.

June 2020

Goals & Plans

Mon **1** Fire	
Tue **2** Water	
Wed **3** Water	
Thur **4** Earth	
Fri **5** Earth	
Sat **6** Metal	
Sun **7** Metal	

June 2020

	lucky directions	conflicting sign/direction	
Mon **8** Wood	South	**Rat** **North**	*Favorable:* Ceremony, trading. *Avoid:* Wedding, moving to a new house, visiting patients.
Tue **9** Wood	Southeast South	**Ox** **West**	*Favorable:* Wedding, travel, haircut, trading, planting, moving to a new house, setting up a door/bed, activating a statue, dress making. *Avoid:* Funeral.
Wed **10** Water	Northeast Southeast	**Tiger** **South**	*Favorable:* Ceremony, wedding, travel, haircut, starting a business, trading, renovation, moving to a new house, setting up a door, dress making. *Avoid:* Setting up a bed or stove.
Thur **11** Water	Northwest Southeast	**Rabbit** **East**	*Favorable:* Bathing, haircut, house cleaning, fixing street/walkway/wall, ceremony, wedding, setting up a stove. *Avoid:* Travel, funeral.
Fri **12** Earth	Southwest West	**Dragon** **North**	*Favorable:* Ceremony, wedding, travel, starting a construction, starting a business, trading, funeral, moving to a new house, setting up a bed, dress making, activating a statue. *Avoid:* Setting up a stove.
Sat **13** Earth	South West	**Snake** **West**	*Favorable:* Ceremony, bathing, pest control. *Avoid:* **Any major festive event.**
Sun **14** Fire	Southeast North	**Horse** **South**	*Favorable:* House demolition, visiting a doctor. *Avoid:* **Any major festive event.**

June 2020

Goals & Plans

Mon **8** Wood	
Tue **9** Wood	
Wed **10** Water	
Thur **11** Water	
Fri **12** Earth	
Sat **13** Earth	
Sun **14** Fire	

June 2020

	lucky directions	conflicting sign/direction	
Mon **15** Fire	Northeast North	**Goat** **East**	*Favorable:* Ceremony, travel, haircut, pest control, funeral, activating a statue. *Avoid:* Wedding.
Tue **16** Wood	Northwest East	**Monkey** **North**	*Favorable:* Meeting friends, travel, starting a construction, funeral, cremation, setting up a bed/stove. *Avoid:* Wedding, moving to a new house.
Wed **17** Wood	Southwest East	**Rooster** **West**	*Favorable:* Ceremony, fixing walls, pest control, fishing. *Avoid:* Wedding, moving to a new house.
Thur **18** Water	South	**Dog** **South**	*Favorable:* Ceremony, travel, starting a construction, planting, wedding, moving to a new house, setting up a bed/stove/door, dress making. *Avoid:* Funeral, starting a business.
Fri **19** Water	Southeast South	**Pig** **East**	*Favorable:* Moving to a new house, dress making, setting up a door/stove, wedding, adopting animals. *Avoid:* Funeral, setting up a bed.
Sat **20** Metal	Northeast Southeast	**Rat** **North**	*Favorable:* Ceremony, funeral, cremation. *Avoid:* **Any major festive event.**
Sun **21** Metal	Northwest Southeast	**Ox** **West**	*Favorable:* Travel, trading, funeral, removing Feng Shui cures. *Avoid:* **Avoid major festive event.**

June 2020

Goals & Plans

Mon **15** Fire	
Tue **16** Wood	
Wed **17** Wood	
Thur **18** Water	
Fri **19** Water	
Sat **20** Metal	
Sun **21** Metal	

June 2020

	lucky directions	conflicting sign/direction	
Mon **22** Fire	Southwest West	**Tiger** **South**	*Favorable:* Ceremony, wedding, renovation, trading, funeral, moving to a new house, setting up a door, dress making. *Avoid:* Starting a business, travel.
Tue **23** Fire	South West	**Rabbit** **East**	*Favorable:* Bathing, house cleaning, wedding, fixing street/walkway/wall. *Avoid:* Travel, moving to a new house, starting a business.
Wed **24** Wood	Southeast North	**Dragon** **North**	*Favorable:* Ceremony, wedding, travel, starting a construction, starting a business, trading, moving to a new house, setting up a bed/door, funeral, dress making, activating a statue. *Avoid:* none.
Thur **25** Wood	Northeast North	**Snake** **West**	*Favorable:* Ceremony, setting up a bed, visiting a doctor, activating a statue, dress making. *Avoid:* Wedding, travel, moving to a new house.
Fri **26** Earth	Northwest East	**Horse** **South**	*Favorable:* House demolition, house cleaning. *Avoid:* **Avoid major festive event.**
Sat **27** Earth	Southwest East	**Goat** **East**	*Favorable:* Ceremony, starting a business, setting up a bed, funeral. *Avoid:* Wedding, setting up a stove.
Sun **28** Metal	South	**Monkey** **North**	*Favorable:* Meeting friends, travel, renovation, starting a construction, starting a business, trading, funeral, setting up a door/bed, dress making, activating a statue. *Avoid:* Moving to a new house.

51

June 2020

Goals & Plans

Mon **22** Fire	
Tue **23** Fire	
Wed **24** Wood	
Thur **25** Wood	
Fri **26** Earth	
Sat **27** Earth	
Sun **28** Metal	

June - July 2020

	lucky directions	conflicting sign/direction	
Mon **29** Metal	Southeast South	**Rooster** **West**	*Favorable:* Ceremony, setting up a stove, planting. *Avoid:* Funeral, wedding, starting a business.
Tue **30** Fire	Northeast Southeast	**Dog** **South**	*Favorable:* Ceremony, wedding, meeting friends, travel, moving to a new house, setting up a bed/stove, dress making. *Avoid:* Funeral, starting a business.
Wed **1** Fire	Northwest Southeast	**Pig** **East**	*Favorable:* Wedding, starting a construction, setting up a stove, moving to a new house, dress making. *Avoid:* Funeral, cremation.
Thur **2** Water	Southwest West	**Rat** **North**	*Favorable:* Ceremony, funeral, cremation. *Avoid:* Setting up a bed or stove, starting a construction.
Fri **3** Water	South West	**Ox** **West**	*Favorable:* Ceremony, wedding, travel, bathing, starting a construction, starting a business, trading, planting, moving to a new house, setting up a door/bed, dress making, activating a statue. *Avoid:* Funeral, setting up a stove.
Sat **4** Earth	Southeast North	**Tiger** **South**	*Favorable:* Ceremony, travel, starting a business, moving to a new house, setting up a door, funeral, dress making. *Avoid:* Setting up a bed or stove, starting a construction, wedding.
Sun **5** Earth	Northeast North	**Rabbit** **East**	*Favorable:* Ceremony, bathing, haircut, house cleaning, fixing a street/walkway. *Avoid:* Moving to a new house.

June - July 2020

Goals & Plans

Mon **29** Metal	
Tue **30** Fire	
Wed **1** Fire	
Thur **2** Water	
Fri **3** Water	
Sat **4** Earth	
Sun **5** Earth	

July 2020 (Lunar calendar: 5/11 to 6/11/2020)

	lucky directions	conflicting sign/direction	
Mon **6** Metal	Northwest East	**Dragon** **North**	*Favorable:* Ceremony, wedding, starting a construction, activating a statue, travel, setting up a bed/door, moving to a house, funeral. *Avoid:* setting up a stove.
Tue **7** Metal	Southwest East	**Snake** **West**	*Favorable:* Ceremony, travel, dress making, renovation, starting a construction, signing a contract, trading, moving to a new house, setting up a bed/door/stove. *Avoid:* Wedding.
Wed **8** Wood	South	**Horse** **South**	*Favorable:* Haircut, bathing, pest control, funeral. *Avoid:* Wedding, moving to a new house.
Thur **9** Wood	Southeast South	**Goat** **East**	*Favorable:* House demolition. *Avoid:* **Any major festive event.**
Fri **10** Water	Northeast Southeast	**Monkey** **North**	*Favorable:* Travel, setting up a bed, dress making, starting a construction, starting a business, moving to a new house, funeral, wedding, activating a statue. *Avoid:* Visiting sick patients.
Sat **11** Water	Northwest Southeast	**Rooster** **West**	*Favorable:* Wedding, dress making, starting a construction, renovation, moving to a new house, funeral, starting a business, ceremony, setting up a bed/stove, activating a statue. *Avoid:* Visiting sick patients.
Sun **12** Earth	Southwest West	**Dog** **South**	*Favorable:* Ceremony, pest control, adopting animals. *Avoid:* setting up a bed/stove, funeral.

July 2020

Goals & Plans

Mon **6** Metal	
Tue **7** Metal	
Wed **8** Wood	
Thur **9** Wood	
Fri **10** Water	
Sat **11** Water	
Sun **12** Earth	

July 2020

	lucky directions	conflicting sign/direction	
Mon **13** Earth	South West	Pig East	*Favorable:* Ceremony, adopting animals. *Avoid:* Travel, moving to a new house, funeral.
Tue **14** Fire	Southeast North	Rat North	*Favorable:* Ceremony, pest control. *Avoid:* **Any major festive event.**
Wed **15** Fire	Northeast North	Ox West	*Favorable:* Ceremony, meeting friends, travel. *Avoid:* Funeral, wedding.
Thur **16** Wood	Northwest East	Tiger South	*Favorable:* Ceremony, meeting friends, dress making, wedding, starting a construction, renovation, setting up a door, starting a business, trading, funeral. *Avoid:* Moving to a new house.
Fri **17** Wood	Southwest East	Rabbit East	*Favorable:* Ceremony, bathing, house cleaning, activating a statue, travel, wedding, dress making, setting up a bed, starting a business, trading, funeral. *Avoid:* Moving to a new house, starting a construction.
Sat **18** Water	South	Dragon North	*Favorable:* Ceremony, wedding, hunting, fishing. *Avoid:* Funeral, planting, setting up a stove.
Sun **19** Water	Southeast South	Snake West	*Favorable:* Ceremony, bathing. *Avoid:* **Any major festive event.**

July 2020

Goals & Plans

Mon **13** Earth	
Tue **14** Fire	
Wed **15** Fire	
Thur **16** Wood	
Fri **17** Wood	
Sat **18** Water	
Sun **19** Water	

July 2020

	lucky directions	conflicting sign/direction	
Mon **20** Metal	Northeast Southeast	Horse South	*Favorable:* Ceremony, wedding, meeting friends, travel, haircut, dress making, funeral, setting up a bed. *Avoid:* Moving to a new house, starting a business.
Tue **21** Metal	Northwest Southeast	Goat East	*Favorable:* Ceremony, house demolition. *Avoid:* **Any major festive event.**
Wed **22** Fire	Southwest West	Monkey North	*Favorable:* Setting up a bed, starting a business, trading, funeral, activating a statue, travel, wedding, dress making, setting up a door, moving to a new house. *Avoid:* Starting a construction.
Thur **23** Fire	South West	Rooster West	*Favorable:* Wedding, dress making, funeral, ceremony, setting up a door/bed. *Avoid:* Starting a business, moving to a new house.
Fri **24** Wood	Southeast North	Dog South	*Favorable:* Ceremony, setting up a stove. *Avoid:* Setting up a bed, starting a business.
Sat **25** Wood	Northeast North	Pig East	*Favorable:* Ceremony, activating a statue, haircut, dress making, wedding, moving to a new house, setting up a bed/door/stove, starting a business. *Avoid:* Funeral, starting a construction.
Sun **26** Earth	Northwest East	Rat North	*Favorable:* Funeral, cremation, pest control. *Avoid:* **Any major festive event.**

July 2020

Goals & Plans

Mon **20** Metal	
Tue **21** Metal	
Wed **22** Fire	
Thur **23** Fire	
Fri **24** Wood	
Sat **25** Wood	
Sun **26** Earth	

July - August 2020

	lucky directions	conflicting sign/direction	
Mon **27** Earth	Southwest East	Ox West	*Favorable:* Ceremony, wedding, meeting friends, travel, dress making, removing Feng Shui cure, moving to a new house, setting up a bed/door, pest control, adopting animals. *Avoid:* Funeral, wedding.
Tue **28** Metal	South	Tiger South	*Favorable:* Ceremony, bathing, house cleaning, activating a statue, removing Feng Shui cures, wedding, starting a business, funeral. *Avoid:* Moving to a new house, setting up a stove.
Wed **29** Metal	Southeast South	Rabbit East	*Favorable:* Ceremony, bathing, house cleaning, dress making, setting up a bed, starting a business, pest control. *Avoid:* Moving to a new house, wedding.
Thur **30** Fire	Northeast Southeast	Dragon North	*Favorable:* Ceremony, bathing, wedding, fishinig. *Avoid:* Funeral, starting a business.
Fri **31** Fire	Northwest Southeast	Snake West	*Favorable:* Meeting friends, dress making, starting a business, trading, travel, haircut, moving to a new house, setting up a door/bed/stove. *Avoid:* Funeral, cremation.
Sat **1** Water	Southwest West	Horse South	*Favorable:* Bathing, haircut, pest control, ceremony, removing Feng Shui cure, funeral. *Avoid:* Moving to a new house, wedding.
Sun **2** Water	South West	Goat East	*Favorable:* Ceremony, house demolition. *Avoid:* **Any major festive event.**

July - August 2020

Goals & Plans

Mon **27** Earth	
Tue **28** Metal	
Wed **29** Metal	
Thur **30** Fire	
Fri **31** Fire	
Sat **1** Water	
Sun **2** Water	

August 2020 (Lunar calendar: 6/12 to 7/13/2020)

	lucky directions	conflicting sign/direction	
Mon **3** Earth	Southwest North	Monkey North	*Favorable:* Travel, dress making, starting a business, funeral, actiavting a statue, wedding, moving to a new house, setting up a bed/door/stove. *Avoid:* Starting a construction.
Tue **4** Earth	Northeast North	Rooster West	*Favorable:* Ceremony, dress making, starting a business, moving to a new house, setting up a door/bed/stove. *Avoid:* Wedding, starting a construction, visiting patients.
Wed **5** Metal	Northwest East	Dog South	*Favorable:* Ceremony, pest control, adopting animals, setting up a stove. *Avoid:* Funeral.
Thur **6** Metal	Southwest East	Pig East	*Favorable:* Ceremony, hiarcut, starting a business. *Avoid:* Moving to a new house, wedding.
Fri **7** Wood	South	Rat North	*Favorable:* Funeral, ceremony, starting a construction, starting a business, activating a statue. *Avoid:* Funeral, visiting sick patients.
Sat **8** Wood	Southeast South	Ox West	*Favorable:* Ceremony, haircut, wedding, pest control, funeral. *Avoid:* Activating a statue.
Sun **9** Water	Northeast Southeast	Tiger South	*Favorable:* Wedding, travel, bathing, house cleaning, ceremony. *Avoid:* Starting a construction, setting up a bed.

August 2020

Goals & Plans

Mon **3** Earth	
Tue **4** Earth	
Wed **5** Metal	
Thur **6** Metal	
Fri **7** Wood	
Sat **8** Wood	
Sun **9** Water	

August 2020

	lucky directions	conflicting sign/direction	
Mon **10** Water	Northwest Southeast	**Rabbit East**	*Favorable:* Ceremony, bathing, haircut, house cleaning, funeral, removing Feng Shui cures, dress making. *Avoid:* Moving to a new house, setting up a stove.
Tue **11** Earth	Southwest West	**Dragon North**	*Favorable:* Meeting friends, dress making, planting, pest control, adopting animals, activating a statue, wedding. *Avoid:* Funeral, starting a construction.
Wed **12** Earth	South West	**Snake West**	*Favorable:* Ceremony, wedding, meeting friends, travel, moving, bathing, dress making, adopting animals, starting a business. *Avoid:* Funeral, cremation.
Thur **13** Fire	Southeast North	**Horse South**	*Favorable:* Ceremony, wedding, travel, dress making, renovation, starting a construction, planting, funeral, activating a statue, moving to a new house, setting up a door/bed. *Avoid:* none.
Fri **14** Fire	Northeast North	**Goat East**	*Favorable:* Ceremony, pest control, planting, hunting, funeral. *Avoid:* **Any major festive event.**
Sat **15** Wood	Northwest East	**Monkey North**	*Favorable:* House demolition. *Avoid:* **Any major festive event.**
Sun **16** Wood	Southwest East	**Rooster West**	*Favorable:* Ceremony, meeting friends, travel, dress making, wedding, renovation, moving to a new house, setting up a door, funeral. *Avoid:* Setting up a bed/stove.

August 2020

Goals & Plans

Mon **10** Water	
Tue **11** Earth	
Wed **12** Earth	
Thur **13** Fire	
Fri **14** Fire	
Sat **15** Wood	
Sun **16** Wood	

August 2020

| --- | --- | --- | --- |
Mon **17** Water	South	**Dog** **South**	*Favorable:* Ceremony, starting a construction, starting a business, trading, planting, funeral, activating a statue, wedding. *Avoid:* Moving to a new house, setting up a stove.
Tue **18** Water	Southeast South	**Pig** **East**	*Favorable:* Ceremony, wedding, meeting friends, moving, dress making, renovation, starting a construction, starting a business, trading planting, setting up a door/stove/bed. *Avoid:* Travel, funeral.
Wed **19** Metal	Northeast Southeast	**Rat** **North**	*Favorable:* Ceremony, travel, wedding, dress making, starting a construction, setting up a bed, starting a business, trading, planting. *Avoid:* Moving to a new house.
Thur **20** Metal	Northwest Southeast	**Ox** **West**	*Favorable:* Ceremony, dress making, wedding, moving to a new house, setting up a bed/stove/door, funeral. *Avoid:* Travel, planting.
Fri **21** Fire	Southwest West	**Tiger** **South**	*Favorable:* Travel, bathing, dress making, house cleaning, adopting aanimals, ceremony, wedding, funeral. *Avoid:* Setting up a bed/stove.
Sat **22** Fire	South West	**Rabbit** **East**	*Favorable:* Ceremony, bathing, dress making, house cleaning, funeral, adopting animals, setting up a bed. *Avoid:* Moving to a new house, wedding.
Sun **23** Wood	Southeast North	**Dragon** **North**	*Favorable:* Wedding, travel, moving, dress making, renovation, starting a business, trading, planting, activating a statue, setting up a door/bed. *Avoid:* Funeral, setting up a stove.

August 2020

Goals & Plans

Mon **17** Water	
Tue **18** Water	
Wed **19** Metal	
Thur **20** Metal	
Fri **21** Fire	
Sat **22** Fire	
Sun **23** Wood	

August 2020

	lucky directions	conflicting sign/direction	
Mon **24** Wood	Northeast North	**Snake** **West**	*Favorable:* Ceremony, bathing, fixing street/walkway/wall. *Avoid:* **Any major festive event.**
Tue **25** Earth	Northwest East	**Horse** **South**	*Favorable:* Ceremony, travel bathing, dress making, renovation, starting a construction, starting a business, trading moving to a new house, setting up a door/bed. *Avoid:* Funeral, wedding.
Wed **26** Earth	Southwest East	**Goat** **East**	*Favorable:* Funeral, pest control. *Avoid:* **Any major festive event.**
Thur **27** Metal	South	**Monkey** **North**	*Favorable:* Bathing, house demolition, visiting a doctor. *Avoid:* **Any major festive event.**
Fri **28** Metal	Southeast South	**Rooster** **West**	*Favorable:* Ceremony, wedding, travel, dress making, starting a business, trading, funeral, activating a statue, moving to a new house. *Avoid:* Setting up a bed/stove.
Sat **29** Fire	Northeast Southeast	**Dog** **South**	*Favorable:* Ceremony, wedding, dress making, renovation, starting a construction, moving to a new house, setting up a stove, funeral. *Avoid:* Setting up a door, planting.
Sun **30** Fire	Northwest Southeast	**Pig** **East**	*Favorable:* Wedding, starting a business, trading, ceremony, activating a statue, dress making, setting up a bed/stove. *Avoid:* Funeral, planting.

August 2020

Goals & Plans

Mon **24** Wood	
Tue **25** Earth	
Wed **26** Earth	
Thur **27** Metal	
Fri **28** Metal	
Sat **29** Fire	
Sun **30** Fire	

August - September 2020

Mon 31 Water	Southwest West	Rat North	*Favorable:* Ceremony, activating a statue, travel, dress making, wedding, meeting friends, starting a construction, setting up a bed. *Avoid:* Funeral, moving to a new house.
Tue 1 Water	South West	Ox West	*Favorable:* Ceremony, travel, dress making, wedding, renovation, starting a construction, moving to a new house, setting up a bed/door, funeral. *Avoid:* Activating a statue, setting up a stove.
Wed 2 Earth	Southeast North	Tiger South	*Favorable:* Ceremony, meeting friends, travel, moving, bathing, dress making, starting a business, funeral, setting up a door/stove. *Avoid: Wedding,* Setting up a bed.
Thur 3 Earth	Northeast North	Rabbit East	*Favorable:* Bathing, haircut, house cleaning, funeral, removing Feng Shui cures, ceremony. *Avoid:* Wedding, moving to a new house.
Fri 4 Metal	Northwest East	Dragon North	*Favorable:* Meeting friends, planting, pest control, adopting animals. *Avoid:* Funeral, wedding.
Sat 5 Metal	Southwest East	Snake West	*Favorable:* Ceremony, bathing, fixing street/walkway/wall, setting up a stove. *Avoid:* Wedding, funeral, cremation.
Sun 6 Wood	South	Horse South	*Favorable:* Ceremony, wedding, travel, dress making, renovation, starting a construction, funeral, moving to a new house, setting up a bed/door. *Avoid:* Activating a statue.

August - September 2020

Goals & Plans

Mon **31** Water	
Tue **1** Water	
Wed **2** Earth	
Thur **3** Earth	
Fri **4** Metal	
Sat **5** Metal	
Sun **6** Wood	

September 2020 (Lunar calendar: 7/14 to 8/14/2020)

	lucky directions	conflicting sign/direction	
Mon **7** Wood	Southeast South	Goat East	*Favorable:* Ceremony, pest control, planting, funeral, removing Feng Shui cures, travel, starting a construction, activating a statue, wedding, setting up a stove, starting a business. *Avoid:* Moving to a new house.
Tue **8** Water	Northeast Southeast	Monkey North	*Favorable:* Bathing, pest control, funeral. *Avoid:* Wedding, moving to a new house, visiting patients.
Wed **9** Water	Northwest Southeast	Rooster West	*Favorable:* Ceremony, house demolition. *Avoid:* **Any major festive event,** visiting sick patients.
Thur **10** Earth	Southwest West	Dog South	*Favorable:* Ceremony, dress making, reovation, starting a construction, setting up a door/bed, moving to a new house, trading, planting, funeral. *Avoid:* Wedding, setting up a stove.
Fri **11** Earth	South West	Pig East	*Favorable:* Ceremony, wedding, dress making, renovation, starting a construction, starting a business, trading, activating a statue, moving to a new house, setting up a door/bed. *Avoid:* Funeral, setting up a stove.
Sat **12** Fire	Southeast North	Rat North	*Favorable:* Ceremony, pest control. *Avoid:* Moving to a new house.
Sun **13** Fire	Northeast North	Ox West	*Favorable:* Ceremony, pest control, hunting. *Avoid:* **Any major festive event.**

September 2020

Mon **7** Wood	
Tue **8** Water	
Wed **9** Water	
Thur **10** Earth	
Fri **11** Earth	
Sat **12** Fire	
Sun **13** Fire	

September 2020

Day	lucky directions	conflicting sign/direction	
Mon **14** Wood	Northwest East	**Tiger** **South**	*Favorable:* Ceremony, dress making, trading, funreal, travel, wedding, renovaion, starting a construction, setting up a door/stove, moving. *Avoid:* Activating a statue, setting up a bed.
Tue **15** Wood	Southwest East	**Rabbit** **East**	*Favorable:* Ceremony, bathing, house cleaning, travel, trading. *Avoid:* Funeral, starting a construction.
Wed **16** Water	South	**Dragon** **North**	*Favorable:* Ceremony, travel, bathing, haircut, dress making, renovation, starting a construction, house cleaning, planting, removing Feng Shui cures, wedding, setting up a bed. *Avoid:* Funeral, moving to a new house.
Thur **17** Water	Southeast South	**Snake** **West**	*Favorable:* Ceremony, bathing, removing Feng Shui cures, activating a statue, haircut, setting up a stove, starting a business, pest control. *Avoid:* Wedding, funeral.
Fri **18** Metal	Northeast Southeast	**Horse** **South**	*Favorable:* Ceremony, bathing, fixing street/walkway/wall. *Avoid:* Wedding, moving to a new house.
Sat **19** Metal	Northwest Southeast	**Goat** **East**	*Favorable:* Ceremony, wedding, travel, dress making, starting a construction, starting a business, funeral, activating a statue, moving to a new house, setting up a bed/stove/door. *Avoid:* none.
Sun **20** Fire	Southwest West	**Monkey** **North**	*Favorable:* Bath, pest control, activating a statue, wedding, meeting friends, setting up a door, funeral. *Avoid:* Moving to a new house, setting up a stove.

September 2020

Mon **14** Wood	
Tue **15** Wood	
Wed **16** Water	
Thur **17** Water	
Fri **18** Metal	
Sat **19** Metal	
Sun **20** Fire	

September 2020

	lucky directions	conflicting sign/direction	
Mon **21** Fire	South West	**Rooster West**	*Favorable:* Ceremony, bathing, house demolition. *Avoid:* **Any major festive event.**
Tue **22** Wood	Southeast North	**Dog South**	*Favorable:* Ceremony, dress making, starting a business, trading. *Avoid:* Wedding, moving to a new house.
Wed **23** Wood	Northeast North	**Pig East**	*Favorable:* Ceremony, dress making, renovation, starting a construction, starting a business, trading, planting, visiting a doctor, moving to a new house, setting up a door/bed/stove. *Avoid:* Funeral, wedding.
Thur **24** Earth	Northwest East	**Rat North**	*Favorable:* Ceremony, haircut, dress making. *Avoid:* Funeral, moving to a new house, visiting patients.
Fri **25** Earth	Southwest East	**Ox West**	*Favorable:* Ceremony, removing Feng Shui cures. *Avoid:* **Any major festive event.**
Sat **26** Metal	South	**Tiger South**	*Favorable:* Ceremony, bathing, dress making, planting, funeral, wedding, rennovation, starting a construction, setting up a stove. *Avoid:* Moving to a new house, activating a statue.
Sun **27** Metal	Southeast South	**Rabbit East**	*Favorable:* Ceremony, bathing, house cleaning, travel. *Avoid:* Moving to a new house, setting up a door.

September 2020

Mon **21** Fire	
Tue **22** Wood	
Wed **23** Wood	
Thur **24** Earth	
Fri **25** Earth	
Sat **26** Metal	
Sun **27** Metal	

September - October 2020

	lucky directions	conflicting sign/direction	
Mon **28** Fire	Northeast Southeast	Dragon North	*Favorable:* Ceremony, travel, bathing, haircut, house cleaning, planting, activating a statue, dress making, wedding, renovation, starting a construction, setting up a bed. *Avoid:* Funeral, setting up a door.
Tue **29** Fire	Northwest Southeast	Snake West	*Favorable:* Ceremony, wedding, travel, bathing, dress making, renovation, starting a business, trading, activating a statue, moving to a new house, setting up a bed/stove. *Avoid:* Funeral, starting a construction.
Wed **30** Water	Southwest West	Horse South	*Favorable:* Ceremony, bathing, fixting street/walkway. *Avoid:* Wedding, moving to a new house.
Thur **1** Water	South West	Goat East	*Favorable:* Dress making, renovation, starting a construction, trading, travel, moving to a new house, setting up a door, planting, funeral. *Avoid:* Wedding.
Fri **2** Earth	Southeast North	Monkey North	*Favorable:* Activating a statue, dress making, starting a construction, funeral, cremation. *Avoid:* Moving to a new house, wedding.
Sat **3** Earth	Northeast North	Rooster West	*Favorable:* House demoliton, visiting a doctor. *Avoid:* **Any major festive event.** Visting sick patients.
Sun **4** Metal	Northwest East	Dog South	*Favorable:* Ceremony, wedding, tavel, renovation, starting a construction, planting, funeral, moving to a new house, setting up a bed/door/stove. *Avoid:* Starting a business.

September - October 2020

Goals & Plans

Mon **28** Fire	
Tue **29** Fire	
Wed **30** Water	
Thur **1** Water	
Fri **2** Earth	
Sat **3** Earth	
Sun **4** Metal	

October 2020 _(Lunar calendar: 8/15 to 9/15/2020)_

	lucky directions	conflicting sign/direction	
Mon **5** Metal	Southwest East	Pig East	_Favorable:_ Ceremony, wedding, renovation, starting a construction, planting, activating a statue, setting up a door/bed/stove. _Avoid:_ Funeral, moving to a new house.
Tue **6** Wood	South	Rat North	_Favorable:_ Ceremony, pest control, haircut, wedding, meeting friends. _Avoid:_ Moving to a new house, setting up a stove, visiting sick patients.
Wed **7** Wood	Southeast South	Ox West	_Favorable:_ Ceremony, meeting friends. _Avoid:_ **Any major festive events.**
Thur **8** Water	Northeast Southeast	Tiger South	_Favorable:_ Ceremony, travel, dress making, starting a construction, starting a business, planting, wedding, setting up a stove, moving to a new house. _Avoid:_ Funeral.
Fri **9** Water	Northwest Southeast	Rabbit East	_Favorable:_ Bathing, haircut, house cleaning, pest control, ceremony, dress making, setting up a stove, funeral. _Avoid:_ planting, wedding.
Sat **10** Earth	Southwest West	Dragon North	_Favorable:_ Ceremony, wedding, travel, dress making, activating a statue, moving to a new house, setting up a door/bed, starting a business, trading. _Avoid:_ Setting up a stove, funeral.
Sun **11** Earth	South West	Snake West	_Favorable:_ Bathing, house cleaning, ceremony, travel, removing Feng Shui cures, haircut, dress making, meeting freinds, setting up a bed, starting a business, trading. _Avoid:_ Wedding, moving to a new house.

October 2020

Goals & Plans

Mon **5** Metal	
Tue **6** Wood	
Wed **7** Wood	
Thur **8** Water	
Fri **9** Water	
Sat **10** Earth	
Sun **11** Earth	

October 2020

	lucky directions	conflicting sign/direction	
Mon **12** Fire	Southeast North	Horse South	*Favorable:* Ceremony, bathing, haircut, meeting friends, setting up a bed, starting a business, trading. *Avoid:* Wedding, moving to a new house.
Tue **13** Fire	Northeast North	Goat East	*Favorable:* Ceremony, fixing street/walkway/walls. *Avoid:* **Any major festive event.**
Wed **14** Wood	Northwest East	Monkey North	*Favorable:* Pest control, funeral. *Avoid:* **Any major festive event.**
Thur **15** Wood	Southwest East	Rooster West	*Favorable:* Ceremony, wedding, dress making, starting a construction, starting a business, trading, funeral, activating a statue, moving to a new house, setting up a bed/door/stove. *Avoid:* none.
Fri **16** Water	South	Dog South	*Favorable:* House demolition. *Avoid:* **Any major festive event.**
Sat **17** Water	Southeast South	Pig East	*Favorable:* Ceremony, wedding, meeting friends, moving, setting up a bed/door, dress making, renovation, starting a construction, hunting, planting, trading. *Avoid:* Funeral, cremation, wedding.
Sun **18** Metal	Northeast Southeast	Rat North	*Favorable:* Wedding, dress making, renovation, starting a construction, funeral, ceremony, activating a statue, moving to a new house, setting up a bed/stove/door. *Avoid:* Starting a business, travel.

October 2020

Mon **12** Fire	
Tue **13** Fire	
Wed **14** Wood	
Thur **15** Wood	
Fri **16** Water	
Sat **17** Water	
Sun **18** Metal	

October 2020

	lucky directions	conflicting sign/direction	
Mon **19** Metal	Northwest Southeast	**Ox** **West**	*Favorable:* Ceremony, hunting, pest control. *Avoid:* Funeral, wedding.
Tue **20** Fire	Southwest East	**Tiger** **South**	*Favorable:* Ceremony, wedding, travel, activating a statue, signing a contract, moving to a new house, setting up a door. *Avoid:* Funeral, starting a business.
Wed **21** Fire	South East	**Rabbit** **East**	*Favorable:* Bathing, house cleaning, pest control, ceremony, dress making, wedding, setting up a bed, funeral. *Avoid:* Setting up a stove.
Thur **22** Wood	Southeast North	**Dragon** **North**	*Favorable:* Building houses for animals. *Avoid:* **Any major festive event.**
Fri **23** Wood	Northeast North	**Snake** **West**	*Favorable:* Bathing, haircut, house cleaning. *Avoid:* Wedding, funeral, starting a construction.
Sat **24** Earth	Northwest East	**Horse** **South**	*Favorable:* Ceremony, bathing, activating a statue, haircut, meeting friends, setting up a bed, starting a business, funeral. *Avoid:* Wedding, moving to a new house.
Sun **25** Earth	Southwest East	**Goat** **East**	*Favorable:* Ceremony, building houses for animals. *Avoid:* **Any major festive event.**

October 2020

Goals & Plans

Mon **19** Metal	
Tue **20** Fire	
Wed **21** Fire	
Thur **22** Wood	
Fri **23** Wood	
Sat **24** Earth	
Sun **25** Earth	

October 2020

	lucky directions	conflicting sign/direction	
Mon **26** Metal	South	Monkey North	*Favorable:* Hunting, fishing, funeral. *Avoid:* **Any major festive event.**
Tue **27** Metal	Southeast South	Rooster West	*Favorable:* Ceremony, wedding, travel, dress making, funeral, moving to a new house, setting up a door/bed/stove. *Avoid:* Starting a business, starting a construction.
Wed **28** Fire	Northeast Southeast	Dog South	*Favorable:* Ceremony, bathing, house demolition, removing Feng Shui cures. *Avoid:* **Any major festive event.**
Thur **29** Fire	Northwest Southwest	Pig East	*Favorable:* Ceremony, setting up a bed, hunting, signing a acontract, dress making, meeting friends. *Avoid:* Travel, planting.
Fri **30** Water	Southwest West	Rat North	*Favorable:* Ceremony, wedding, travel, dress making, starting a business, funeral, activating a statue, moving to a new house, setting up a bed/door. *Avoid:* Starting a construction, setting up a stove.
Sat **31** Water	South West	Ox West	*Favorable:* Ceremony, hunting, pest control. *Avoid:* Starting a business, setting up a stove.
Sun **1** Earth	Southeast North	Tiger South	*Favorable:* Ceremony, meeting friends, travel, bathing, haircut, house cleaning, removing Feng Shui cures, activating a statue, visiting a doctor. *Avoid:* Wedding, starting a business.

October 2020

Goals & Plans

Mon **26** Metal	
Tue **27** Metal	
Wed **28** Fire	
Thur **29** Fire	
Fri **30** Water	
Sat **31** Water	
Sun **1** Earth	

November 2020 (Lunar calendar: 9/16 to 10/16/2020)

	lucky directions	conflicting sign/direction	
Mon **2** Earth	Northeast North	**Rabbit** **East**	*Favorable:* Bathing, haircut, house cleaning, ceremony, removing Feng Shui cure, setting up a bed/stove/door, pest control. *Avoid:* Wedding, activating a statue.
Tue **3** Metal	Northwest East	**Dragon** **North**	*Favorable:* Ceremony, meeting friends, dress making. *Avoid:* Funeral ,wedding.
Wed **4** Metal	Southwest East	**Snake** **West**	*Favorable:* Ceremony, travel, moving, bathing, dress making, starting a business, setting up a bed. *Avoid:* Wedding, setting up a stove.
Thur **5** Wood	South	**Horse** **South**	*Favorable:* Ceremony, bathing, activating a statue, haircut, meeting friends, starting a business, trading, funeral. *Avoid:* Wedding, setting up a stove.
Fri **6** Wood	Southeast South	**Goat** **East**	*Favorable:* Fixing street and walkway. *Avoid:* Any major festive event.
Sat **7** Water	Northeast Southeast	**Monkey** **North**	*Favorable:* Dress making, renovation, starting a construction, starting a business, trading, funeral. *Avoid:* Wedding, moving to a new house, visiting patients.
Sun **8** Water	Northwest Southeast	**Rooster** **West**	*Favorable:* Ceremony, travel, dress making, renovation, starting a construction, starting a business, funeral, moving to a new house, setting up a bed/stove. *Avoid:* Wedding, visiting sick patients.

November 2020

Goals & Plans

Mon **2** Earth	
Tue **3** Metal	
Wed **4** Metal	
Thur **5** Wood	
Fri **6** Wood	
Sat **7** Water	
Sun **8** Water	

November 2020

	lucky directions	conflicting sign/direction	
Mon **9** Earth	Southwest West	Dog South	*Favorable:* Bathing, haircut, pest control, removing Feng Shui cures, ceremony, activating a statue, wedding, dress making, setting up a door/bed, funeral. *Avoid:* Starting a business.
Tue **10** Earth	South West	Pig East	*Favorable:* Ceremony, house demolition. *Avoid:* **Any major festive event.**
Wed **11** Fire	Southeast North	Rat North	*Favorable:* Ceremony, hunting, wedding, dress making, moving, setting up a door/bed/stove, funeral. *Avoid:* Starting a construction.
Thur **12** Fire	Northeast North	Ox West	*Favorable:* Ceremony, trading, planting, removing Feng Shui cures, wedding, starting a construction. *Avoid:* Wedding, travel.
Fri **13** Wood	Northwest East	Tiger South	*Favorable:* Ceremony, house cleaning, pest control, hunting. *Avoid:* **Any major festive event.**
Sat **14** Wood	Southwest East	Rabbit East	*Favorable:* Ceremony, bathing, activating a statue, travel, removing Feng Shui cures, haircut, wedding, starting a construction, setting up a bed, planting,. *Avoid:* Moving to a new house, setting up a stove.
Sun **15** Water	South	Dragon North	*Favorable:* Setting up a bed, pest control. *Avoid:* Funeral, wedding.

November 2020

Goals & Plans

Mon **9** Earth	
Tue **10** Earth	
Wed **11** Fire	
Thur **12** Fire	
Fri **13** Wood	
Sat **14** Wood	
Sun **15** Water	

November 2020

	lucky directions	conflicting sign/direction	
Mon **16** Water	Southeast South	Snake West	*Favorable:* Ceremony, bathing. *Avoid:* Wedding, starting a business.
Tue **17** Metal	Northeast Southeast	Horse South	*Favorable:* Ceremony, wedding, moving, dress making, renovation, starting a construction, funeral, activating a statue, setting up a door. *Avoid:* Moving to a new house, starting a business.
Wed **18** Metal	Northwest Southeast	Goat East	*Favorable:* Ceremony, haircut, meeting friends, pest control. *Avoid:* Moving to a new house, wedding.
Thur **19** Fire	Southwest West	Monkey North	*Favorable:* Wedding, travel, dress making, renovation, starting a construction, starting a business, trading, planting, funeral, moving to a new house, setting up a door. *Avoid:* Ceremony, setting up a stove.
Fri **20** Fire	South West	Rooster West	*Favorable:* Travel, haircut, starting a construction, renovation, starting a business, trading, funeral, ceremony, moving to a new house, setting up a door/bed. *Avoid:* Wedding, setting up a stove.
Sat **21** Wood	Southeast North	Dog South	*Favorable:* Bathing, haircut, hunting, removing Feng Shui cures, ceremony, wedding, dress making, setting up a bed, funeral. *Avoid:* Starting a business.
Sun **22** Wood	Northeast North	Pig East	*Favorable:* Ceremony, house demolition, removing Feng Shui cures. *Avoid:* **Any major festive event.**

November 2020

Goals & Plans

Mon **16** Water	
Tue **17** Metal	
Wed **18** Metal	
Thur **19** Fire	
Fri **20** Fire	
Sat **21** Wood	
Sun **22** Wood	

November 2020

	lucky directions	conflicting sign/direction	
Mon **23** Earth	Northwest East	Rat North	*Favorable:* Ceremony, travel, dress making, renovation, starting a construction, funeral, activating a statue, starting a business, moving to a new house, setting up a bed/stove. *Avoid:* Wedding, setting up a door.
Tue **24** Earth	Southwest East	Ox West	*Favorable:* Ceremony, meeting friends, dress making, renovation, starting a construction, trading setting up a bed/stove, planting, funeral. *Avoid:* Wedding, moving to a new house.
Wed **25** Metal	South	Tiger South	*Favorable:* Ceremony, bathing, house cleaning, pest control, hunting. *Avoid:* **Any major festive event.**
Thur **26** Metal	Southeast South	Rabbit East	*Favorable:* Ceremony, bathing, haircut, activating a statue, travel, dress making, wedding, starting a construction, starting a business, trading, planting, setting up a bed. *Avoid:* Setting up a stove.
Fri **27** Fire	Northeast Southeast	Dragon North	*Favorable:* Ceremony, travel, wedding, starting a construction, pest control, funeral. *Avoid:* Activating a statue, setting up a door.
Sat **28** Fire	Northwest Southeast	Snake West	*Favorable:* Ceremony, bathing, travel. *Avoid:* Setting up a stove.
Sun **29** Water	Southwest West	Horse South	*Favorable:* Travel, bathing, haircut, wedding, dress making, renovation, starting a construction, setting up a door, moving to a new house, starting a business, funeral. *Avoid:* Planting.

95

November 2020

Goals & Plans

Mon **23** Earth	
Tue **24** Earth	
Wed **25** Metal	
Thur **26** Metal	
Fri **27** Fire	
Sat **28** Fire	
Sun **29** Water	

November - December 2020

	lucky directions	conflicting sign/direction	
Mon **30** Water	South West	Goat East	*Favorable:* Ceremony. *Avoid:* **Any major festive event.**
Tue **1** Earth	Southeast North	Monkey North	*Favorable:* Wedding, meeting friends, travel, dress making, starting a business, trading, activating a statue, moving to a new house, setting up a door/bed. *Avoid:* Wedding, funeral.
Wed **2** Earth	Northeast North	Rooster West	*Favorable:* Ceremony, travel, dress making, renovation, starting a construction, funeral, moving to a new house, setting up a bed/stove/door. *Avoid:* Wedding, visiting sick patients.
Thur **3** Metal	Northwest East	Dog South	*Favorable:* Ceremony, meeting friends, wedding, dress making, planting, funeral, activating a statue, travel, renovation, moving to a new house, setting up a door/bed. *Avoid:* Starting a business, setting up a stove.
Fri **4** Metal	Southwest East	Pig East	*Favorable:* House demolition. *Avoid:* **Any major festive event.**
Sat **5** Wood	South	Rat North	*Favorable:* Ceremony, meeting friends, dress making, bathing, activating a statue, travel, wedding, renovation, starting a construction, moving to a new house, setting up a bed/stove. *Avoid:* Funeral.
Sun **6** Wood	Southeast South	Ox West	*Favorable:* Ceremony, wedding, meeting friends, adopting animals, removing Feng Shui cures, bathing, haircut, planting, funeral. *Avoid:* Starting a business, setting up a stove.

November - December 2020

Goals & Plans

Mon **30** Water	
Tue **1** Earth	
Wed **2** Earth	
Thur **3** Metal	
Fri **4** Metal	
Sat **5** Wood	
Sun **6** Wood	

December 2020 (Lunar calendar: 10/17 to 11/17/2020)

Day	lucky directions	conflicting sign/direction	
Mon **7** Water	Northwest Southeast	Tiger South	*Favorable:* Ceremony, travel, dress making, funeral, renovation, setting up a stove. *Avoid:* Wedding, moving to a new house.
Tue **8** Water	Northwest Southeast	Rabbit East	*Favorable:* Ceremony, bathing, haircut, house cleaning, pest control, hunting, setting up a bed/stove. *Avoid:* Starting a business, planting.
Wed **9** Earth	Southwest West	Dragon North	*Favorable:* Ceremony, meeting friends, dress making, renovaition, starting a construction, planting, activating a statue, setting up a bed/door. *Avoid:* Wedding, moving to a new house.
Thur **10** Earth	South West	Snake West	*Favorable:* Ceremony, bathing, dress making, planting, pest control, adopting animals, wedding, renovation, starting a construction, moving to a new ouse, setting up a door. *Avoid:* Funeral, cremation.
Fri **11** Fire	Southeast North	Horse South	*Favorable:* Ceremony. *Avoid:* Any major festieve event.
Sat **12** Fire	Northeast North	Goat East	*Favorable:* Ceremony, travel, wedding, trading, dress making, renovation, starting a construction, moving to a new house, setting up a door/bed, planting. *Avoid:* Funeral, setting up a stove.
Sun **13** Wood	Northwest East	Monkey North	*Favorable:* Meeting friends, dress making, renovation, starting a business, trading, planting, activating a statue, haircut, setting up a bed, funeral. *Avoid:* Moving to a new house, setting up a stove/door.

December 2020

Goals & Plans

Mon **7** Water	
Tue **8** Water	
Wed **9** Earth	
Thur **10** Earth	
Fri **11** Fire	
Sat **12** Fire	
Sun **13** Wood	

December 2020

	lucky directions	conflicting sign/direction	
Mon **14** Wood	Southwest East	**Rooster** **West**	*Favorable:* Ceremony. *Avoid:* **Any major festive event.**
Tue **15** Water	South	**Dog** **South**	*Favorable:* Ceremony, travel, dress making, renovation, starting a construction, planting, funeral, moving to a new house, setting up a door/bed. *Avoid:* Wedding.
Wed **16** Water	Southeast South	**Pig** **East**	*Favorable:* Ceremony, pest control, hunting, activating a statue, dress making, wedding, meeting friends, moving to a new house, setting up a bed. *Avoid:* Starting a business, funeral.
Thur **17** Metal	Northeast Southeast	**Rat** **North**	*Favorable:* Ceremony, house demolition. *Avoid:* **Any major festive event.**
Fri **18** Metal	Northwest Southeast	**Ox** **West**	*Favorable:* Ceremony, hunting, haircut, wedding, setting up a bed, moving, funeral. *Avoid:* Setting up a door.
Sat **19** Fire	Southwest West	**Tiger** **South**	*Favorable:* Wedding, travel, bathing, haircut, dress making, funeral, ceremony, activating a statue, setting up a door, moving to a new house. *Avoid:* Setting up a bed/stove.
Sun **20** Fire	South West	**Rabbit** **East**	*Favorable:* Ceremony, bathing, house cleaning, pest control, dress making, starting a business, hunting, planting. *Avoid:* Funeral, wedding.

December 2020

Goals & Plans

Mon **14** Wood	
Tue **15** Water	
Wed **16** Water	
Thur **17** Metal	
Fri **18** Metal	
Sat **19** Fire	
Sun **20** Fire	

December 2020

	lucky directions	conflicting sign/direction	
Mon **21** Wood	Southeast North	**Dragon** **North**	*Favorable:* Ceremony, meeting friends, dress making, renovation, starting a construction, planting, removing Feng Shui cures, setting up a door. *Avoid:* Wedding, setting up a bed.
Tue **22** Wood	Northeast North	**Snake** **West**	*Favorable:* Bathing, dress making, pest control, travel, haircut, moving. *Avoid:* Moving to a new house.
Wed **23** Earth	Northwest East	**Horse** **South**	*Favorable:* Training animals. *Avoid:* **Any major festive event.**
Thur **24** Earth	Southwest East	**Goat** **East**	*Favorable:* Ceremony, wedding, travel, bathing, haircut, trading, house cleaning, dress making, setting up a bed, planting. *Avoid:* Activating a statue, setting up a stove.
Fri **25** Metal	South	**Monkey** **North**	*Favorable:* Travel, dress making, renovation, starting a business, trading, funeral, planting, setting up a door/bed. *Avoid:* Wedding, setting up a stove.
Sat **26** Metal	Southeast South	**Rooster** **West**	*Favorable:* Fixing street/walkway. *Avoid:* **Any major festive event.**
Sun **27** Fire	Northeast South	**Dog** **South**	*Favorable:* Ceremony, wedding, travel, dress making, renovation, starting a construction, activating a statue, moving to a new house, setting up a door/bed, planting, funeral. *Avoid:* Setting up a door/stove.

December 2020

Mon **21** Wood	
Tue **22** Wood	
Wed **23** Earth	
Thur **24** Earth	
Fri **25** Metal	
Sat **26** Metal	
Sun **27** Fire	

December 2020 - January 2021

	lucky directions	conflicting sign/direction	
Mon **28** Fire	Northwest Southeast	Pig East	*Favorable:* Ceremony, activating a statue, bathing, haircut, wedding, dress making, meeting friends, renovation, starting a construction, moving to a new house, setting up a bed/door/stove. *Avoid:* Funeral, starting a business.
Tue **29** Water	Southwest West	Rat North	*Favorable:* Ceremony, house demolition. *Avoid:* **Any major festive event.**
Wed **30** Water	South West	Ox West	*Favorable:* Ceremony, activating a statue, travel, wedding, renovation, starting a construction, setting up a bed, starting a business, trading, funeral, hunting. *Avoid:* Setting up a door/stove.
Thur **31** Earth	Southeast North	Tiger South	*Favorable:* Travel, bathing, haircut, dress making, ceremony, renovation, moving to a new house, setting up a stove/door. *Avoid:* Wedding, setting up a bed.
Fri **1** Earth	Northeast North	Rabbit East	*Favorable:* Bathing, haircut, house cleaning hunting, planting, pest control. *Avoid:* Wedding, moving to a new house.
Sat **2** Metal	Northwest East	Dragon North	*Favorable:* Ceremony, meeting friends, dress making, renovation, starting a construction, planting, setting up a door/bed, adopting animals. *Avoid:* Moving to a new house, wedding.
Sun **3** Metal	Southwest East	Snake West	*Favorable:* Bathing, dress making, pest control, renovation, starting a construction, setting up a stove, planting. *Avoid:* Wedding, setting up a bed.

December 2020 - January 2021

Goals & Plans

Mon **28** Fire	
Tue **29** Water	
Wed **30** Water	
Thur **31** Earth	
Fri **1** Earth	
Sat **2** Metal	
Sun **3** Metal	

January 2021 (Lunar calendar: 11/18 to 12/19/2020)

	lucky directions	conflicting sign/direction	
Mon **4** Wood	South	Horse South	*Favorable:* Starting a business, funeral. *Avoid:* Wedding, setting up a stove.
Tue **5** Wood	Southwest South	Goat East	*Favorable:* Ceremony, wedding, travel, haircut, renovation, starting a construction, planting, moving to a new house, setting up a bed. *Avoid:* Funeral, starting a business.
Wed **6** Water	Northeast Southeast	Monkey North	*Favorable:* Wedding, dress making, renovation, starting a construction, setting up a bed/door, funeral, starting a business. *Avoid:* Ceremony, visiting sick patients.
Thur **7** Water	Northwest Southeast	Rooster West	*Favorable:* Ceremony, removing Feng Shui cures, wedding, travel, moving, setting up a bed/door, funeral, starting a business. *Avoid:* Moving to a new house, setting up a stove.
Fri **8** Earth	Southwest West	Dog South	*Favorable:* Ceremony, dress making, meeting friends, fixing street/walkway. *Avoid:* Wedding, funeral.
Sat **9** Earth	South West	Pig East	*Favorable:* Ceremony. *Avoid:* Funeral, wedding.
Sun **10** Fire	Southeast North	Rat North	*Favorable:* Ceremony, travel, wedding, dress making, renovation, setting up a bed, moving, funeral, bathing, haircut, hunting. *Avoid:* Starting a business, setting up a stove.

January 2021

Goals & Plans

Mon **4** Wood	
Tue **5** Wood	
Wed **6** Water	
Thur **7** Water	
Fri **8** Earth	
Sat **9** Earth	
Sun **10** Fire	

January 2021

Mon **11** Fire	Northeast North	Ox West	*Favorable:* Ceremony, bathing, house demolition. *Avoid:* **Any major festive event.**
Tue **12** Wood	Northwest East	Tiger South	*Favorable:* Ceremony, travel, dress making, renovation, starting a construction, moving to a new house, activating a statue, setting up a door/stove, funeral. *Avoid:* Setting up a bed.
Wed **13** Wood	Southwest East	Rabbit East	*Favorable:* Ceremony, bathing, haircut, house cleaning, removing Feng Shui cures, funeral. *Avoid:* **Any major festive event.**
Thur **14** Water	South	Dragon North	*Favorable:* Ceremony, hunting, pest control. *Avoid:* Starting a business, setting up a bed.
Fri **15** Water	Southeast South	Snake West	*Favorable:* Activating a statue, bathing, haircut, meeting friends. *Avoid:* Funeral, travel.
Sat **16** Metal	Northeast Southeast	Horse South	*Favorable:* Ceremony, dress making, funeral, renovation, setting up a door/stove, trading, adopting aninals. *Avoid:* Wedding, activating a statue.
Sun **17** Metal	Northwest Southeast	Goat East	*Favorable:* Ceremony, meeting friends, removing Feng Shui cures. *Avoid:* **Any major festive event.**

January 2021

Goals & Plans

Mon **11** Fire	
Tue **12** Wood	
Wed **13** Wood	
Thur **14** Water	
Fri **15** Water	
Sat **16** Metal	
Sun **17** Metal	

January 2021

	lucky directions	conflicting sign/direction	
Mon **18** Fire	Southwest West	**Monkey** **North**	*Favorable:* Dress making, wedding, meeting friends, trading, moving to a new house, setting up a bed, funeral. *Avoid:* Ceremony, setting up a stove.
Tue **19** Fire	South West	**Rooster** **West**	*Favorable:* Ceremony, travel, wedding, dress making, meeting friends, setting up a bed, starting a business, trading, funeral. *Avoid:* Setting up a stove.
Wed **20** Wood	Southeast North	**Dog** **South**	*Favorable:* Fixing street/walkway, *Avoid:* **Any major festive event.**
Thur **21** Wood	Northeast North	**Pig** **East**	*Favorable:* Meeting friends, ceremony, activating a statue, moving to a new house, setting up a bed/stove. *Avoid:* Funeral.
Fri **22** Earth	Northwest East	**Rat** **North**	*Favorable:* Ceremony, wedding, travel, bathing haircut, dress making, funeral, setting up a bed. *Avoid:* Starting a construction, setting up a stove, visiting patients.
Sat **23** Earth	Southwest East	**Ox** **West**	*Favorable:* Ceremony, house demolition, removing Feng Shui cures. *Avoid:* **Any major festive event.**
Sun **24** Metal	South	**Tiger** **South**	*Favorable:* Activating a statue, ceremony, bathing, haircut, starting a business, travel, meeting friends, wedding, trading, funeral. *Avoid:* Moving to a new house, starting a construction.

January 2021

Goals & Plans

Mon **18** Fire	
Tue **19** Fire	
Wed **20** Wood	
Thur **21** Wood	
Fri **22** Earth	
Sat **23** Earth	
Sun **24** Metal	

January 2021

	lucky directions	conflicting sign/direction	
Mon **25** Metal	Southeast South	**Rabbit** **East**	*Favorable:* Ceremony, removing Feng Shui cures. *Avoid:* **Any major festive event.**
Tue **26** Fire	Northeast Southeast	**Dragon** **North**	*Favorable:* Ceremony, pest control, hunting, wedding, dress making, setting up a stove. *Avoid:* Starting a business, setting up a bed.
Wed **27** Fire	Northwest Southeast	**Snake** **West**	*Favorable:* Ceremony, dress making, starting a business, removing Feng Shui cures, haircut, wedding, moving to a new house, setting up a door/bed/stove. *Avoid:* Wedding.
Thur **28** Water	Southwest West	**Horse** **South**	*Favorable:* Ceremony, bathing, funeral, dress making, setting up a bed, trading. *Avoid:* Wedding, setting up a stove.
Fri **29** Water	South West	**Goat** **East**	*Favorable:* Ceremony, removing Feng Shui cures. *Avoid:* **Any major festive event.**
Sat **30** Earth	Southeast North	**Monkey** **North**	*Favorable:* Dress making, wedding, meeting friends, moving to a new house, setting up a door/bed, starting a business, trading, funeral. *Avoid:* Travel, setting up a stove.
Sun **31** Earth	Northeast North	**Rooster** **West**	*Favorable:* Ceremony, dress making, wedding, setting up a bed, starting a business, pest control, adopting animals. *Avoid:* Funeral, setting up a stove, visiting sick patients.

January 2021

Goals & Plans

Mon **25** Metal	
Tue **26** Fire	
Wed **27** Fire	
Thur **28** Water	
Fri **29** Water	
Sat **30** Earth	
Sun **31** Earth	

February 2021 (Lunar calendar: 12/20/2020 to 1/17/2021)

	lucky directions	conflicting sign/direction	
Mon **1** Metal	Northwest East	Dog South	*Favorable:* Ceremony, starting a business, dress making, setting up a bed, funeral. *Avoid:* Setting up a stove, planting.
Tue **2** Metal	Southwest East	Pig East	*Favorable:* Ceremony, meeting friends, adopting animals. *Avoid:* Wedding, starting a construction.
Wed **3** Wood	South	Rat North	*Favorable:* Ceremony, dress making, meeting friends, funeral. *Avoid:* Wedding, moving to a new house.
Thur **4** Wood	Southeast South	Ox West	*Favorable:* Ceremony, wedding, travel, meeting friends, funeral. *Avoid:* Moving to a new house.
Fri **5** Water	Northeast Southeast	Tiger South	*Favorable:* Ceremony, bathing, house cleaning, demolition. *Avoid:* **Any major festive event.**
Sat **6** Water	Northwest Southeast	Rabbit East	*Favorable:* Ceremony, bathing, funeral, activating a statue, travel, renovation, starting a construction, setting up a door. *Avoid:* Wedding, moving to a new house.
Sun **7** Earth	Southwest West	Dragon North	*Favorable:* Ceremony, removing Feng Shui cures, pest control, hunting, funeral. *Avoid:* **Any major festive event.**

February 2021

Goals & Plans

Mon **1** Metal	
Tue **2** Metal	
Wed **3** Wood	
Thur **4** Wood	
Fri **5** Water	
Sat **6** Water	
Sun **7** Earth	

February 2021

	lucky directions	conflicting sign/direction	
Mon **8** Earth	South West	**Snake West**	*Favorable:* Ceremony, meeting friends, dress making, travel, moving, renovation, starting a construction, starting a business, trading, planting, activating a statue, setting up a bed/door. *Avoid:* Funeral, moving to a new house.
Tue **9** Fire	Southeast North	**Horse South**	*Favorable:* Ceremony, bathing, activating a statue, haircut, wedding, dress making, meeting friends, starting a construction, starting a business, trading, planting. *Avoid:* Funeral, moving to a new house.
Wed **10** Fire	Northeast North	**Goat East**	*Favorable:* Ceremony, dress making, setting up a bed, stove, pest control, funeral. *Avoid:* Wedding, moving to a new house.
Thur **11** Wood	Northwest East	**Monkey North**	*Favorable:* Meeting friends, dress making, starting a business, trading, adopting animals, funeral. *Avoid:* Moving to a new house.
Fri **12** Wood	Southwest East	**Rooster West**	*Favorable:* Ceremony, dress making, signing agreement, wedding, moving to a new house, meeting friends, travel. *Avoid:* none.
Sat **13** Water	South	**Dog South**	*Favorable:* Moving to a new house, ceremony. *Avoid:* Funeral, setting up a bed/stove.
Sun **14** Water	Southeast South	**Pig East**	*Favorable:* Fixing up a street/walkway, setting up a stove. *Avoid:* **Any major festive event.**

February 2021

Goals & Plans

Mon **8** Earth	
Tue **9** Fire	
Wed **10** Fire	
Thur **11** Wood	
Fri **12** Wood	
Sat **13** Water	
Sun **14** Water	

February 2021

	lucky directions	conflicting sign/direction	
Mon **15** Metal	Northeast Northeast	**Rat** **North**	*Favorable:* Activating a statue, signing a contract, dress making, starting a construction, setting up a bed/door, meeting friends, travel, adopting animals. *Avoid:* Funeral, planting, setting up a stove.
Tue **16** Metal	Northwest Northeast	**Ox** **West**	*Favorable:* Ceremony, signing a contract, dress making, wedding, moving to a new house, setting up a bed/door, funeral, removing a Feng Shui cure, fishing. *Avoid:* Starting a business, starting a construction, setting up a stove.
Wed **17** Fire	Southwest West	**Tiger** **South**	*Favorable:* House demolition, visitng a doctor. *Avoid:* **Any major festive event.**
Thur **18** Fire	South West	**Rabbit** **East**	*Favorable:* Signing a contract, wedding, starting a construction, miving to a new house, funeral, travel, bathing, renovation, removing Feng Shui cures, setting up a door. *Avoid:* Setting up a bed/stove.
Fri **19** Wood	Southeast North	**Dragon** **North**	*Favorable:* Funeral, fishing. *Avoid:* Wedding, moving to a new house, setting up a stove.
Sat **20** Wood	Northeast North	**Snake** **West**	*Favorable:* Ceremony, bathing, signing a contract, dress making, setting up a bed, starting a business, trading, fishing, adopting animals. *Avoid:* Funeral, setting up a stove.
Sun **21** Earth	Northwest East	**Horse** **South**	*Favorable:* Ceremony, bathing, signing a contract, dress making, starting a business, trading, travel. *Avoid:* Funeral, moving to a new house, setting up a stove.

February 2021

Goals & Plans

Mon **15** Metal	
Tue **16** Metal	
Wed **17** Fire	
Thur **18** Fire	
Fri **19** Wood	
Sat **20** Wood	
Sun **21** Earth	

February 2021

	lucky directions	conflicting sign/direction	
Mon **22** Earth	Southwest East	Goat East	*Favorable:* Ceremony, funeral. *Avoid:* **Any major festive event.**
Tue **23** Metal	South	Monkey North	*Favorable:* Removing Feng Shui cures, dress making, setting up a bed, trading, adopting animals, funeral. *Avoid:* Wedding, travel, starting a construction, moving to a new house.
Wed **24** Metal	Southeast South	Rooster West	*Favorable:* Wedding, setting up a bed, activating a statue, travel, ceremony, starting a construction, removing Feng Shui cures, meeting friends, starting a business, trading, moving to a new house, funeral. *Avoid:* none.
Thur **25** Fire	Northeast Northeast	Dog South	*Favorable:* Wedding, activating a statue, meeting friends, setting up a bed, visiting a doctor. *Avoid:* Moving to a new house, starting a business, funeral.
Fri **26** Fire	Northwest Northeast	Pig East	*Favorable:* Fixing a street/walkway, removing Feng Shui cures, setting up a stove. *Avoid:* Travel, planting, funeral, setting up a door.
Sat **27** Water	Southwest West	Rat North	*Favorable:* Removing Feng Shui cures, bathing. *Avoid:* **Any major festive event.**
Sun **28** Water	South West	Ox West	*Favorable:* Wedding, ceremony, travel, removing Feng Shui cures, starting a construction, moving to a new house, setting up a bed, planting, adopting animals, funeral. *Avoid:* Starting a business, setting up a stove.

February 2021

Goals & Plans

Mon **22** Earth	
Tue **23** Metal	
Wed **24** Metal	
Thur **25** Fire	
Fri **26** Fire	
Sat **27** Water	
Sun **28** Water	

10 Year Plan

| 2020 |
| 2021 |
| 2022 |
| 2023 |
| 2024 |
| 2025 |
| 2026 |
| 2027 |
| 2028 |

10 Year Plan

2020	
2021	
2022	
2023	
2024	
2025	
2026	
2027	
2028	

2020 Monthly Goals

January	February
March	April
May	June

2020 Monthly Goals

July	August
September	October
November	December

2021 Monthly Goals

January	February

March	April

May	June

2021 Monthly Goals

July	August
September	October
November	December

Notes

Notes

Printed in Great Britain
by Amazon